"Hershey"
Congressional Medal of Honor Recipient
Korean War
Hiroshi "Hershey" Miyamura

by
Dale E. Malone & Charles R. Woodson

Front Cover U.S. Medal of Honor, Digital Image Source Unknown
Back cover photograph of Hiroshi "Hershey" Miyamura, Photographer Unknown
Cover redesigned by C. Woodson 2010

Copyright 2002 by Dale E. Malone and Charles R. Woodson

First Edition Published September, 2002
Second Edition Published May, 2010

Published by Sunwood Entertainment Corporation
http://www.sunwoodentertainment.com

TABLE OF CONTENTS

ACKNOWLEDGMENTS

From the Publisher & Authors

We dedicate this book to all of the heroes of our country, who live, and have lived, each day in service, and who remind us all of the strength of the human spirit and the strength of our nation.

Special thanks and appreciation to Hershey and Terry Miyamura for entrusting us with his personal history, and to his sister Michiko Yoshida, the family historian, who entrusted us with her time and input and numerous family photo albums, and to the entire Miyamura family and its extensions for all of their support throughout the years it took to complete this project!

From Hiroshi Miyamura

To Dale Malone, Charles (Chuck) Woodson and Sherry Thomas for making this book a reality. Thank you so very much.

All of the members of my family also thank you so much for all the time and effort you have all put into this book.

Chuck and Sherry, it is patriots like you, who make America what it is, the greatest country in the world. I know all of my fellow Japanese-Americans are proud to be able to say, "We are Americans!"

FORWARD

This is the amazing story of a quiet, shy, American young man, born of immigrant parents, who grew up to face a daunting challenge in his mid 20s. A monumental challenge, the result of which put a small town in New Mexico, USA, on the map of the nation's eyes and catapulted this self-effacing youth into the history books. To hear him tell of this historic event, he did little at all and was quite surprised at the notoriety that befell him after his release from a Chinese-Communist POW camp after an internment of over two-and-a-half years.

Sit back and learn that heroes are not necessarily specially gifted individuals, anxiously awaiting some supreme obstacle to surmount, but rather they represent ordinary human beings who, when faced with a sequence of circumstances that most of us would quail in fear at, they instead step into the breach and perform tasks so courageous as to motivate General officers to rise, stand at attention, and salute them with honor and pride for their accomplishments. Hiroshi "Hershey" Miyamura will relate his own story, of how he won this nation's highest military honor, as he "distinguished himself by conspicuous gallantry and intrepidity in action at the risk of his life above and beyond the call of duty in action against the enemy." He will accomplish this with assistance from articles, interviews, and anecdotes from friends and relatives.

Hershey

1

Hershey was sitting in the shade at home in Gallup, New Mexico, drinking a frosty iced tea, and he was gathering wool.

It was one of those really spectacular evenings in New Mexico, where the combination of dust and the cloud patterns resulted in a breathtaking sunset that painted a panorama of glorious hues of orange, tangerine, saffron, red, purple, and peach.

It was always his thought that, "I really should capture one of these sunsets on film," but Hershey had been consistently deficient at this task. So, he took

another sip of his tea, sighed, and nodded his head at the panoramic display.

Well, not to worry he thought, someone would take a great photograph of the splendor, and it would be printed in the newspaper, or he could pick it up off the web while browsing his favorite regional sites.

The evening was cooling off and Hershey was planning on going fishing in the morning, up to Tsalie Lake, northwest in Arizona, in the middle of the Navaho Indian Reservation. He would go with his long-time buddy, the ex-mayor of Gallup, Edward Muñoz. Eddie would drive the ninety or so miles and they would be leaving at about five a.m. to insure they arrived at their secret fishing spot by sunup. Hershey remembered that at one time Eddie thought he would like to race in the local car-racing events. He rebuilt a '37-Ford chassis and rebuilt the engine. When it was finished, a friend of his wanted to try it out on the oval dirt track and crashed it! Eddie couldn't afford the expense of fixing it up again, and that spelled the end of his racing dreams.

Hershey

Hershey was looking forward to catching some fat Rainbow trout, or possibly a German Brown trout or two or three, and he knew that Eddie would again be bottom fishing for catfish and trying his damnedest to hook his elusive nemesis "Carlos the Catfish."

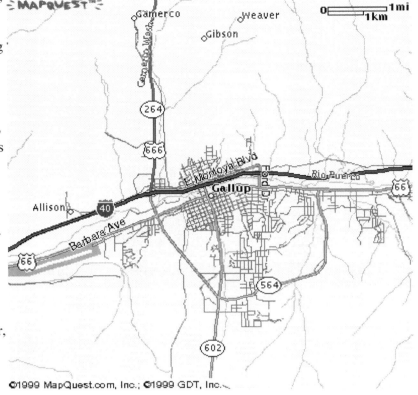

©1999 MapQuest.com, Inc.; ©1999 GDT, Inc.

Hershey chuckled to himself as he thought of this and realized that there probably was no 25-pound catfish. But that Eddie was always telling stories about figments of his imagination. Tall tales of how he had Carlos hooked, but good, then the wily scoundrel had pulled out the hook and swam off, headed for the southern end of the lake. Or, how he was pulling the "cold-blooded aquatic vertebrate of the class Pisces," into the boat when Carlos somehow lunged, got off the hook, flopped out of the boat, and plunged back into the lake, drenching Eddie with his splash, and then, how he came up and looked Eddie right in the eye, winked at him, and seemed to be laughing at his failure to catch and keep him.

Hershey, in all the times they had gone fishing together had never seen "hide nor hair" of the slimy denizen of the deep. But it did make for good chit-chat on the drive up and back.

Eddie's trailer and 14-foot boat, with its electric motor, were already hooked up to Ed's 4WD GMC pick-up, and Hershey's wife Terry had packed a lunch for him, placing it in the refrigerator to keep overnight. It consisted of a Denver sandwich, which Hershey finds delicious. If it's a ham or salami sandwich, she usually gives him a couple of hard-boiled eggs and cheese to go with it. She adds an apple or a banana. Then of course, she is sure to include the sweet morsels he really enjoys, especially if it's chocolate-flavored.

Hershey

As he was thinking along these lines, Hershey's thoughts, as they were wont to do as he got older, strayed back to the Korean peninsula on that fateful day in April, 1951, more than 50 years ago…

"My heavy-machine-gun squad of thirteen soldiers was dug-in on a hill overlooking the Imjin River and just across it was the camp of the Chinese Communists. We were just north of the 38th parallel [n.b. This line of Latitude approximates the border between North and South Korea]. There were huge bonfires and a horde of enemy infantry was encamped along the banks of the river.

"We began to see troop movements and other activity along the river's edge as the enemy began to cross the river. They reformed on our side of the Imjin and at about one hour before midnight the quiet of the night was shattered by the blaring of bugles, beating of drums, screaming of unintelligible epithets, and an extensive tumult from the teeming masses, and it sounded like they were pounding on garbage-can lids with clubs.

Hershey

"The attack that we had all feared had commenced..."

Hershey

2

The sound of Amtrak's east-bound passenger train which traveled just below Hershey's house in Gallup, New Mexico, broke into his reverie and he was jogged back into his past. His thoughts were directed to just how he had ended up on that mountainside in the cruddiest "police action" imaginable. Every Chinese infantryman in the world was charging up the hill towards him and his squad.

It was almost three years exactly into the Second World War when…

"I got my draft notice in October of 1943 and I was inducted into the Army on January 13th, 1944. I was transported by a black-smoke-belching diesel bus, where I spent a week at Ft. Bliss, in El Paso, Texas and got all my necessary shots, my 'You're in the Army now,' indoctrination, uniforms, and other paraphernalia. Then I boarded a train with the other recruits to journey to Camp Blanding, in St. Augustine, Florida.

"There were only two companies of Nisei [n.b. refers to a person born in America of parents who had emigrated from Japan] and we were told we were going to receive 17-weeks of basic training there. We were in the 232nd B Recruit Training Course.

Hershey

"After basic training we journeyed, again by train, to Camp Shelby for advanced infantry training in Meridian, Mississippi.

"Upon completion of our training, just before the train was pulling out of the station and heading for the embarkation base for Europe, seven of us were pulled off and we were told we weren't going with the unit. We were informed at

that time that it was because we

weren't yet nineteen years old. I discovered that you had to be nineteen to be eligible to be sent overseas.

"They assigned us to various companies, I was assigned to Dog Company of the 100th Battalion of the 442nd Regimental Combat Team RCT]. I was going to be trained to become a heavy-weapons machine gun operator. Thus, my training was on how to operate and care for the .30 caliber, water-cooled machine gun.

"After thirteen more weeks of training, we boarded a train destined for Ft. George G. Meade, Maryland, where we underwent an equipment inspection and a medical examination prior to embarkation to Europe. The Army doctor, a colonel, who was examining me said that I had a hernia and he wanted to know if it was bothering me.

Hershey

No. 713 "LAST CHANCE" NIGHT CLUB, CAMP PATRICK HENRY, VA.

"I said, 'No, it isn't and I didn't even know that I had a hernia.' But he said he was going to send me back to my unit in Camp Shelby and have me operated on to have it taken care of.

"I then got my orders to report all the way back to the Camp Shelby Hospital. After the operation, I spent seventeen days in bed. Then two more weeks recuperating. During that time, because I could do no lifting, I was assigned as the jeep driver for the Chaplin of the Four-Four-Two.

No. 711 DEBARKS FIRST MEAL, CAMP PATRICK HENRY, VA.

Hershey

"It was now time for my fateful third attempt to be transferred to a staging area overseas. As another unit had just completed basic training, we again were loaded aboard a train with their complement and traveled to Camp Patrick Henry, in Virginia, where our final briefings were held. Then we boarded a train for transport to a Liberty ship docked at Newport, Virginia.

Hershey

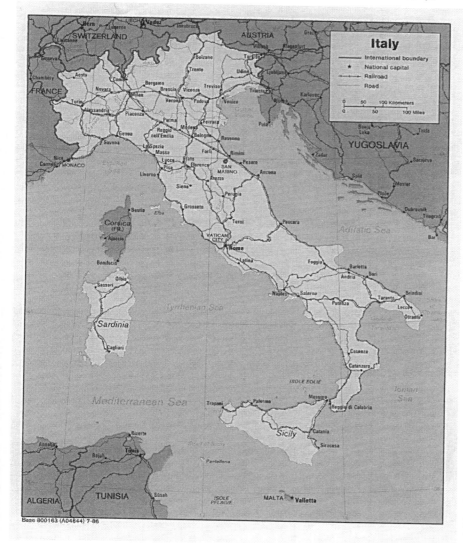

The journey and the ship were so unremarkable, that I cannot remember the name of it, and we steamed for Europe. Five days out of Naples, Italy, the war in Europe ended.

"There were rumors flying around that the ship was going to turn about and proceed to the Pacific Theater. But we were then told we would join the Four-Four-Two that was processing German prisoners-of-war at an airfield named Gaiato, near Bologna, in Northern Italy.

"I was asked during an interview: 'You said there were rumors when the war was declared over in Europe that you were going to go to the Pacific with the other [Japanese-American] troops. Did you guys have any reservations about fighting in the Pacific?'

"My reply was an emphatic no! Because our outlook, as a whole, was just like any other American. I was brought up as an American. My thoughts were the furthest away from being an enemy of our country. I didn't classify myself as a Japanese from Japan. I classified myself as an American from New Mexico. That was the way I was brought up by my father.

Hershey

"We finally arrived in port at Naples and our unit was posted up near the Swiss border. We had to ride trucks all the way up to the border. We finally joined the unit and then proceeded to perform guard duty to guard U.S. Medical installations. There were a lot of German POW camps throughout Italy. They kept moving us from town-to-town just to guard these German POWs.

"Then we were again advised that we were going to be deploying to the Pacific, and that we had to undergo some further training for the war in the Pacific Theater. Once again, before we got into it, the war ended in the Pacific. We were then informed that we were going be to guarding military installations throughout Italy. I spent some time in Lecco, in Northern Italy, and then

in Leghorn, further south, guarding medical supply depots.

Hershey

"It was during my time in Northern Italy that I got a seven-day pass and went to visit Switzerland on R&R [n.b. military jargon for Rest & Recuperation, Relaxation, Recreation, and Romance] with some buddies. We saw some really spectacularly beautiful mountain country and met some very nice people. We visited Bern, Lucerne, Zurich and Lugano. Having gotten used to traveling by train ever since I was inducted into the military, we again did our traveling throughout Europe by train. We went through the Swiss Alps and some of the most incredibly lovely villages there. The people were very friendly to us Japanese-Americans. They even opened their homes to us. It was interesting to note the differences between the French, Swiss, and Italian people and the variety in the places we visited along our journey.

"After returning from the R&R, I was again stationed here and there, all over Southern Italy, then after some months, I was informed that we were going to return stateside with the Regimental Colors. We departed from, I believe it was Livorno, Italy, on another Liberty ship, the Wilson Victory.

"Believe me, everyone was happy to be heading back home to America.

Hershey

"When we arrived in New York Harbor, we were met by tugboats with fountain-like sprays of water, all kinds of small planes buzzing around and a flotilla of small boats in the harbor. It was very exciting to all of us G.I.'s.

"When we docked we were very surprised to see all the banners and the multitude of people waiting for us. After our debarkation, we were told that we were going to be going to Washington, D.C. and our unit would be reviewed by the President of the United States, who at that time was Harry S. Truman.

"We traveled to Washington, D.C. where we then marched in a military parade down Constitution Avenue in the rain, to a parade-ground near the Capitol where we marched in review, and were presented with another Presidential Unit Citation banner for our Regimental Colors. President Truman stood out in the rain to inspect us, and that fact impressed me more than anything else about the whole event.

Hershey

"Looking back, I guess the patriotism that stayed with me all of my life came from the boys of the 100th/442nd. They taught me what true patriotism really is. When you think about volunteering to serve your country while your family is interned back at home because you and your family are thought to 'possibly' be an enemy is quite incredible. The 100th/442nd is one of the most decorated unit of its size that fought in World War II and these boys risked their lives for America. That is patriotism! They are my heroes.

"From Washington D.C. I was transported back to Fort George G. Meade, Maryland. There I got my separation papers. I was then advised that I had an 'opportunity' to join the Army Reserves, and I did... for a three year hitch. That was in June of 1946.

"During 1946 and 1947, I was in Milwaukee, Wisconsin where I attended the Milwaukee School of Engineering, a private school, to study refrigeration and air-conditioning under the G.I. Bill.

"I went to class five days a week from eight a.m. to three p.m. The local area around where the school was located was very green and beautiful, but it was very humid in the summer and colder than a deep coal-miner's butt in the winter. Not a very comfortable climate for someone who had been raised in Gallup, New Mexico. I tell you, the humidity was terrible!"

Hershey

It was during this period of time, while Hershey was on a return home between classes, that he first met his wife-to-be Tsuruko 'Terry' Tsuchimori, who was born in Los Angeles in 1925, and had lived in Winslow, Arizona. Her family, during the crazed period after the war started, was rounded up and transferred to the prisoner internment camp at Poston, Arizona, along with 18,000 other Japanese and Japanese-American citizens. Terry's family had moved from Winslow, Arizona to Los Angeles at the outbreak of the war. Her father had lost his job because of the prejudice that had begun against American's of Japanese descent. He was working for the Santa Fe Railroad. Then, after having been released from the internment camp with her family, she moved to Gallup.

"After we met and when I returned to Milwaukee, we continued to carry on our courtship through correspondence, even though we didn't really get along that well right off. I had actually been writing to her, after being initially introduced to her through the match-making efforts of my sister Suzi, while I was going to school.

"After a year in Milwaukee, I returned to Gallup for the Christmas holidays. My cousin, Frank, a master-mechanic had just opened up Frank's Auto Repair and he asked me to come and work for him. This is why, instead of returning to refrigeration school, I began working for my cousin Frank.

"Terry and I got married on June 20, 1949, with my best friend and boyhood chum, Amelio DiGregorio, as my best man.

"I mistakenly thought Terry had a lot of money saved because she was working on her own all of those years and I expected to see a big bankroll. [Hershey was laughing while relating this to me.] We got married and I asked to see her bank account and we found out that neither one of us had any money. [More bittersweet laughter] After that I told her, 'Here, try these pants on.' She said, 'But they don't fit!' I then said, 'Now you remember that because I'm the one who wears the pants in this family.' [More laughter followed the relating of this anecdote.]

Hershey

"A year or more had gone by and I was working for my cousin as an auto mechanic. Then, in 1949 we were in a recession and business was awfully slow. I had no intention of reenlisting in the reserves, but one day, a silver-tongued, glib recruiting officer, who had been trying to get me to reenlist for quite a spell said, 'Your three year hitch is up, do you want to reenlist again?' Acting on an impulse, I said, 'Yes, I think I want a change.' I didn't tell Terry about it. I reenlisted for another three years."

That fateful decision would change his life forever and would be the catalyst that would transform him from a quiet, non-assuming young man into what was widely perceived as a prominent celebrity and a national hero.

Hershey's mind was fairly buzzing with all of the memories and the emotions associated with them. It was five days after his second wedding anniversary…

MAP 2

From: Ebb And Flow, November 1950-July 1951
Center of Military History, 1990
By Billy C. Mossman

Hershey

It was early on a Sunday morning in Korea, the 25th of June, 1950, quite like the situation in Pearl Harbor had been nine years earlier when the Japanese had launched their unannounced and unprovoked Naval air attack against the sleeping protectors in Hawaii. It was still dark, around 4 a.m. local time, when the North Koreans and Communist Chinese launched a major assault all along the division between North and South Korea, the 38th parallel. They moved into South Korea, shattering the tenuous peace and after having banged on their war-drums for almost ten years, the so-called Korean "conflict" broke out for real.

From the novel, The Captains: Brotherhood of War Book II, is an excellent description of the breakout of hostilities and the disposition and equipment of the enemy and friendly forces:

The 38th parallel bisects the Korean peninsula. From a point near Ongjin, on the Yellow Sea, to another near Yangyang on the Sea of Japan, the parallel stretches just over 200 miles.

If the forces of the Immun Gun, the Army of the People's Democratic Republic of Korea, had been spread out equally across the 38th parallel, there would have been one Immun Gun soldier every twelve feet. There were 90,000 of them. And one in three of these was a veteran of the Chinese Communist Army, which had just sent Chiang Kai-shek fleeing to the island of Formosa.

They were not, of course, spread out across the line. They were formed in Russian-style military organizations. There were seven infantry divisions, one armored brigade, equipped with the Russian T34 tank which had stopped Germany's best, a separate infantry regiment, a motorcycle regiment, and a brigade of the Border Constabulary, the Bo An Dae, North Korea's version of the Waffen SS.

They had 150 tanks in all, and 200 airplanes, large quantities of 76 mm self-propelled howitzers, and even more 122 mm truck-drawn howitzers. They were "advised" by a large contingent of Russian officers and technicians, and they were equipped with Russian small arms.

They also had boats, and they made two amphibious landings behind the South Korean lines between Samch'ok and the 38th parallel on the Sea of Japan in coordination with an attack by the 5th Infantry Division on the 10th Regiment of the Republic of Korea's (ROK) 8th Infantry Division.

Hershey

22

The 2nd and 7th North Korean Infantry Divisions attacked the understrength ROK 6th Division at Ch'unch'on. The 3rd and 4th North Korean Infantry Divisions, reinforced by the 14th Tank Regiment, attacked the ROK 7th Division at Uijongbu. The North Korean 1st and 6th Infantry Divisions, reinforced by the 203rd Tank Regiment, attacked the ROK 1st "Capitol" Division (less the 17th Infantry Regiment) at Kaesong on the route to Seoul and Inchon. And on the extreme left of the front, that peaceful Sunday morning, the North Korean Border Constabulary Brigade and the 14th Infantry Regiment attacked the ROK 17th Infantry Regiment, which held the Ongjin peninsula on the Yellow Sea.

"Shortly after that, in August, I got recalled into the Army. At the time I was in Delta, Colorado with relatives, enjoying the fishing and scenery in the Western Rocky Mountains. I received my orders to report to Ft. Hood, Texas for a nine-week refresher course."

His wife Terry recalls the dread in her heart the day Hershey was recalled to active service. At the time Hershey was making pretty good money as a mechanic and the future was looking rosy. When the orders came, Hershey assured Terry he wouldn't be going overseas. The army had told him he'd be used as a cadre man training recruits.

"All we did was march all day... continuously... everyday... with a full field pack!"

Ya really gotta love the Army!

"We then boarded a train bound for California, and it came right through Gallup, and for some reason or another, because it was not normally a stop, the train halted at the station, and I asked the Troop Commander of the train if I could run home. At that time, I only lived a short distance away. He said, 'O.K., but when you hear that whistle blow, you better come a-running.'

"There were three of us who ran home, and when we heard the locomotive whistle blow, we ran back. Terry and I did get to spend about 15-minutes together before I left the for the West Coast."

Hershey

When Hershey left Gallup, he continued on to Camp Stoneman, across the bay from San Francisco, in the vicinity of the city of Pittsburg.

On his way, Hershey passed through the Los Angeles area where his brother Kei along with his girlfriend Kimi, who was about seventeen years old at the time, lived. Kimi was reluctant to meet anyone in Kei's family, let alone his big brother. Kimi, who at age nine, had been detained with her family and transported to the prisoner internment camp at Jerome, Arkansas, with 8,500 other Japanese-Americans and Japanese citizens, was somewhat shy. When she was informed that he was going to visit briefly before going north to the Bay area, she chose not to meet him.

On the night before leaving California, on November 16, 1950, Hershey called Terry and informed her that he was not being stationed in California as he had presumed, but was shipping out for Japan.

Hershey was flown from San Francisco, on a commercial flight with a single stop at Wake Island in the Pacific, to the commercial airport in Tokyo, Japan [n.b. Haneda Airport]. Then he was transported by truck to Camp Drake where he boarded a train to Sasebo, Japan.

"We rode a day and a night and I ended up on the Southern island of Kyushu, Japan.

Hershey

"I was told to report to the 3rd Infantry Division, 7th Infantry Regiment, 2nd Battalion, H Company, which was a heavy-weapons company. They were training around Mt. Monji in preparation for deployment to Korea.

"While there, although my father never really talked about his early life in Japan, I knew he was from this part of Japan. Also one of my relatives wrote and said, 'That's the island where your folks lived and where your father is from.' While I was stationed there training, I wrote back and tried to get the names of some of our relatives and find out where they lived. Nobody wrote back in time before I left. I was to find out later, I was only a one-hour train ride from where they lived."

Hershey spent about a month there on Kyushu before his unit boarded another undistinguished transport ship bound for Korea. He departed from the seaport at Fukuoka, Japan and arrived at Wonson harbor, North Korea in November of 1950.

Hershey

3

"Cripes, sitting in the balmy evening in Gallup, I shuddered as I remembered how bitterly cold it was when we arrived at Wonson harbor in North Korea aboard that Liberty ship…

"From there, our Regiment made our way in a northerly deployment, up the North Korean peninsula, until we arrived at our position on a mountain overlooking the Yalu River. We were told to dig-in to the frozen ground there and remain there until told to move. We could easily see the camps of the Chinese troops bivouacked across the river on the North bank of the Yalu. We didn't know what they had in mind, and I don't think our command unit knew either, but I was pretty sure that I would not like what they had planned for me.

"We were dug in on the mountaintop along with the 2nd Battalion, companies E and F. As I remember, the nearest town was a small village named Tarjon-ni. I don't think it is even there any longer. It was bitterly cold where we were and the icy wind out of the northwest was blowing all the time. It was wet and cut right through your 'winter' uniform like it was a fleecy beach costume.

"My first experience with combat occurred there, near Huksari, soon after I arrived in North Korea. The enemy launched a midnight attack on the American hill positions. The battle lasted well into the morning. Suddenly two squads of Yanks – eighteen men in all, myself included – found ourselves isolated on a ridge.

"We tried to make our way down and were met by withering enemy small-arms and artillery fire. We backtracked up to the crest as a flight of American fighter-bombers swooped down with their wing-guns blazing. We frantically waved everything we had, and thankfully, the planes veered off to another target. It was just the diversion needed for me and my comrades to scramble off of that hill.

"Some time later, at another rocky hill, all of a sudden the Chinese crossed the river in a mob and, just like ants out of their hive, they swarmed toward our trenches. We were dug-in on our mountainside and in very short order we were commanded to retreat from our position, but even before we could leave, once again, our own planes began strafing us. I don't know what happened … they were thinking we were overrun, or they thought we were the enemy. I just don't know, I never did find out why they started strafing our positions."

Hershey

Hershey's unit was ordered to go to a regrouping area on the East coast of North Korea. During this period the enemy had overran all the units in the whole Northern part of North Korea. He then began to make his way back to the Port of Hungnam any way he could. Hershey was lucky and happened to get a ride on a tank that was part of a unit that was retreating south, and he got to Hungnam where his unit regrouped.

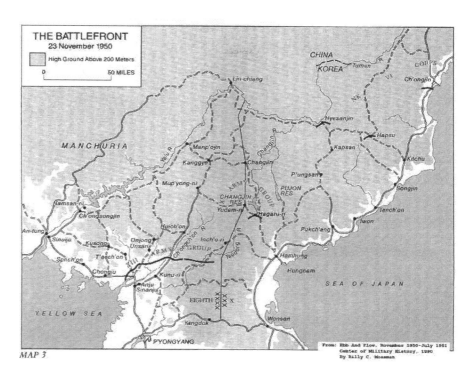

MAP 3

Hershey

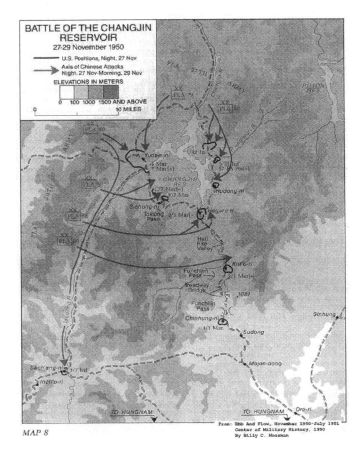

BATTLE OF THE CHANGJIN
RESERVOIR
27-29 November 1950

U.S. Positions, Night, 27 Nov
Axis of Chinese Attacks
Night, 27 Nov-Morning, 29 Nov
ELEVATIONS IN METERS

0   100 1000 1500 AND ABOVE
0   10 MILES

MAP 8

From: Ebb And Flow, November 1950-July 1951
Center of Military History, 1950
By Billy C. Mossman

His unit was then detailed to hold the perimeter because this was also the regrouping area where all of the American ground forces that were being evacuated from the intense battles around the Chosen Reservoir [n.b. Also called the Chosin or Changjin Reservoir] were assembling. At that battleground the Allied forces, numbering approximately 25,000 troops, were attacked by a numerically superior force of the Chinese, who outnumbered them by nearly 100,000 troops.

Hershey

This evacuation area was the Port of Hungnam and the Allied units were withdrawing by boarding Liberty ships there, and later the evacuating troops were even being loaded onto LSTs [n.b. Landing Ship Tank: A flat-bottomed vessel developed during World War II to land troops and cargo on open beaches and was sometimes used as a weapons platform and hospital ship.] Our unit was one of the last ones to evacuate and we boarded a ship out of Hungnam on December 24th, Christmas Eve, 1950."

Hershey

4

Back in Gallup, Hershey's wandering thoughts reflected that at the time he had thought this evacuation was quite a splendid Christmas gift, although the wrapping paper and the container could have benefitted from some better choices. If he only knew what awaited him…

"We steamed for Pusan, on the Southeast coast of South Korea. After docking and forming up, the next thing you know, we were loaded back onto trucks and were again headed back up north. We made our way up north, past Seoul, near the 38th parallel, which had been leveled by our aircraft bombing it.

"Then after a month or so of fighting, after we had advanced deeper into North Korea, we had started withdrawing because the enemy had commenced what was destined to be referred to as their 'Spring Offensive.' We were always grossly outnumbered so we had to withdraw slowly and carefully. On our last retreat, we crossed south over the Imjin River and we were told to 'dig in' and hold our positions for as long as we could. Consequently, that is what we did.

Hershey

"I was placed in charge of our 13-man machine-gun squad. We crossed the Imjin River and we dug-in and I was ordered to have our men cover a portion of the perimeter and I was assigned four extra riflemen to my squad."

The Chinese were engaged in fighting a battle against a modern enemy unlike any they had ever fought before. They still moved all of their army on foot and did not rely on trucks for transport of equipment. Every soldier in each squad had to carry extra rations, ammunition or other equipment that they would need along the way.

"We were dug into our positions, and we had been issued a lot of ammunition. We were heavily armed, and nothing happened for a day or so. But on the evening of the 24th of April, 1951 around midnight we began hearing whistles... banging of metal... blowing bugles... screaming and yelling... a lot of commotion. Then what were obviously hordes of Chinese infantry started swarming up the draw in what has been later described as a human-wave assault.

"We did have flares set up on our perimeter, so when their advance set off a flare or two, we knew they were down in that area just below us, so I gave the orders for the two machine guns to open fire.

Hershey

"Pretty soon the firing ceased and this gunner, my first gunner, came up to me and said, 'It's too hot here. I'm gonna leave!' I almost shot the guy for abandoning his gun. He just got me so mad I went to the gun and began firing it. After a while it jammed on me because it really takes two men to operate that heavy water-cooled machine gun. In the dark and not being able to feed the magazine belt properly, it jammed, so I stuck a grenade in the feed mechanism and blew it up to disable it in case we were overrun."

According to later reports, after running out of grenades, he then exited the safety of his

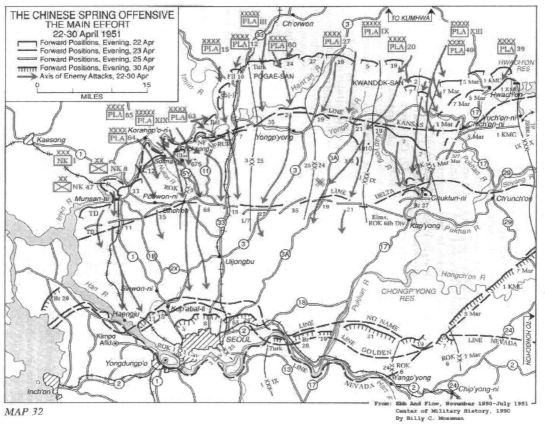

MAP 32

From: Ebb And Flow, November 1950-July 1951
Center of Military History, 1990
By Billy C. Mossman

position and charged the advancing Chinese, armed only with his M-1 rifle with a bayonet attached. He reportedly dispatched ten of the CHICOM [n.b. Chinese Communist] infantrymen in hand-to-hand combat.

"Then I went to the second machine gun position and it was unmanned! I didn't know when or why the team was gone, so I asked the men there. They said they didn't know, but half of my squad was gone and I couldn't figure it out. I guess someone must have given them orders to withdraw but I never did get the word."

Hershey

In a subsequent interview, he related that incoming grenades being lobbed by the attacking Chinese had caused the gunners to have to abandon their machine-gun position.

"After quite a lot of fighting, I realized our position was hopeless now because the enemy had advanced around us and they were now behind us. I told the remaining five men to retreat and I pointed out to them the route to follow. While they retreated, I covered their withdrawal with my M-1 rifle. They exited where the other gun emplacement was dug out and they went out through the opening there and went back out of the area.

"Pretty soon white phosphorus shells were hitting my position, I really didn't know if it was ours. I thought it was ours. I didn't think the Chinese had white phosphorus.

"... I can't actually think or talk about the combat action ... what actually happened ... because I hate to say what actually happened. I just cannot talk about it even now. This is mainly because I was in a different frame of mind at that time because of the circumstances.

Hershey

"I realized then it was time to get out. That is why I was making my way down one of the trenches… you understand that in North Korea, because of the continued fighting up and down the whole Korean peninsula, there were trenches dug all over. On the way back, in one of those trenches, I came face-to-face with one of the enemy soldiers. I could recognize by the shape of his uniform and his hat, in the reflection from muzzle flashes and explosions, that he was a Chinese soldier.

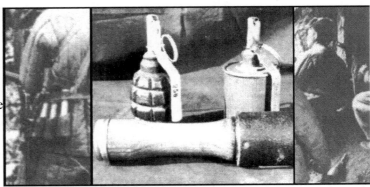

"I could also see that this soldier had a concussion grenade gripped in his hand and I thrust forward and stabbed him with my bayonet. As I withdrew my bayonet, I fired the rifle and shot him. I fell backwards. I was on my back when he tossed the grenade at me. I felt it hit me in the leg so I kicked at it and knocked it back and it rolled back toward him and exploded. Part of that shrapnel hit me in the leg, although I didn't realize it at that time." [n.b. Hershey was later awarded the Purple Heart medal for this battle injury.]

This action was reported as follows in a later interview:

Now he was alone with the enemy.

Hershey jumped into a network of trenches that the Chinese had hacked out for some earlier battle before they lost the terrain. He rounded a corner and crashed into a Chinese with a grenade in his hand. Hershey fired from his hip as he dropped flat. The enemy crumpled and the grenade rolled forward. Hershey kicked it away. An instant later it exploded. A jagged fragment of steel slashed through the flesh of Hershey's right leg, but he wasn't aware of the wound until some time later.

Hershey leaped up. Behind the dead Chinese were others. He charged with bayonet high, slashing and jabbing in a fury. Screaming, the enemy scattered.

Hershey

"I jumped up out of there and started running and crawling. I estimate the distance from the top of this hill to where the barbed-wire entanglement at the base of the hill was located was about 500-yards. But I hadn't known that our troops had set-up this barbed-wire snarl and I ran right smack into it and cut my hand wide open.

"There was a tank sitting there, one of our tanks, right ahead of me there past the barbed wire, just getting ready to pull out, and that is why I really hadn't seen the barbed-wire until I got caught up in it. I was running as fast as I could and trying to flag the tank-crew down. In a way, I guess that was a good thing they did not see me because they might have thought I was the enemy and shot me. Because it was dark, they wouldn't have known who was who out there.

"The tank pulled out, so I crawled under the barbed-wire and then got up and ran another 50-yards or so. Then I dropped to the ground, because I couldn't go anymore. Chinese infantrymen were all over the battlefield there. Where I had fallen down, was a draw or a gully, and I just laid down thinking maybe no one would see me. I don't know how long I laid there, I guess it wasn't more than an hour or so and it was starting to get light. Here comes their troops right by where I was laying quietly and no one stopped to see if I was dead or alive. Pretty soon I heard no more noise and I thought, 'Well, they didn't see me.'

Hershey

"Then next thing you know, I hear a voice. It was a Chinese officer, 'Get up! You're our prisoner. We have a lenient policy, we won't harm you, just follow me.' "

Hershey

5

Oh dear God! The absolute worst nightmare of any soldier! Not to be killed or wounded in combat, but to be captured by an enemy, particularly in that backward part of the world of Communism.

Scuttlebutt [n.b military slang for gossip or a rumor] had been circulating among the troops about the horribly inhumane treatment that the Chinese and North Korean's were reputed to dish-out to captured prisoners...

"Following his orders, I got up and that was when I realized for the first time that I was really hit. I hobbled and followed after him and I had to pass a lot of their troops that were still in the area. All of them were pointing their weapons and gesturing at me in a threatening manner, like they wanted to shoot me. Then the officer took me to an area where there were about eight or nine of my fellow soldiers there, all wounded. I then helped them with first-aid the best I could. My fellow section Sergeant, Sgt. Joseph Annello, was wounded, and between the two of us, we hobbled along together until he finally said, 'I can't make it, I can't go any more.' He said, 'Just set me down here,' which I eventually did, although reluctantly. I thought that once I set him down it would be the last I would see of him."

Hershey, understandably, became quite emotional while relating this incident.

The captives were interrogated during this stop and at subsequent ones.

Hershey

Meanwhile the disappearance of Corporal Miyamura had been noted in several quarters. In H Company, 7th Regiment, Third Division, Miyamura's outfit, the commanding officer heard the circumstances of the squad leader's loss and filed a comprehensive report. It passed from battalion, to regiment, to division, and in due time an investigation was ordered.

When the survivors of his squad had been questioned and all the fragments of information were put together, it was ascertained that Hershey had killed more than 50 of the enemy, many in hand-to-hand combat. He had helped evacuate the wounded and he had covered the withdrawal of his men. When last seen, he had been fighting fiercely against an overwhelming number of enemy soldiers. Corporal Miyamura was recommended forthwith for high military honors.

But the whole story wasn't allowed to reach Hershey's family just then.

In sun-baked Gallup, Terry Miyamura was working at Jay's Super Market when the telegram arrived for her. All of the employees knew Hershey was expected home soon and Terry hadn't heard from her husband for several weeks. As she tore open the yellow envelope, she anticipated word that he was on his way. As Terry read the telegram she began to cry. The other employees realized the telegram was not giving her good news. The entire store was in tears.

The brutally formal message left her stunned. Hershey was missing in action.

It was reported that after his capture, Hershey was marched right past the position that his machine gun crew had defended and he saw 40 to 50 dead enemy soldiers strewn in front of the position that they had defended.

Hershey

"Well then, they put us into a dug-out [n.b. a shelter dug out of the side of a hill] until it really got to be dark and we were told to get out and they tied our arms together, from prisoner-to-prisoner, and we were told to follow them. We had to make our way as best we could. That went on for about two or three days. We were told we were going to follow the Chinese troops south as they advanced, and then we'd pick up more prisoners and would head back for a permanent camp. After about two more weeks we were joined by about twelve or thirteen other American prisoners. Then we started making our way back north to a POW camp.

"We used to walk at night only because I think they were afraid that our air forces would attack us thinking we were an enemy column and they did not want to attract the attack to themselves. But that did not work out because our guys would bomb and strafe at night, and one night they bombed the village we happened to be in, and they dropped napalm. Several of the prisoners got burned by the napalm and one died.

Hershey

"The Chinese eventually decided we would have to take our chances during the daylight hours. All during this time we had not had any medical attention and also we had not eaten for a week or so. The head-sheds [n.b. military slang for the people in charge] then decided that we were going to eat the same emergency rations as the Chinese. They gave us a small sack of finely-ground millet, barley, and rice that we called 'bug dust.' We were told to take pinches of it and drink water with it and it would swell up in your stomach and make you feel full. But you carried your own ration and it had to last you a week. If you finished your ration, you did without until the rations were replenished.

"During that march, which I estimate was about 500 kilometers [n.b. approximately 300 miles, although another prisoner estimates that it must have been almost 400 miles, what with the route that had to be taken to avoid open ground, the mountainous terrain, and the continued harrying of allied air strikes], we lost many of our troops because of the lack of medical attention and first-aid to our wounds, no medicine, and the lack of proper food … and I guess, the will to live. But what kept me going was seeing a young soldier who was in my machine gun company section, who had a good-sized hole in the side of his body and I kept looking at him thinking, 'If he can make it, I can make it.'

"Somewhere along the march we noticed that maggots were forming inside this soldier's wound and I thought for sure he has had it. But we discovered that the maggots were good for him because they ate all the poison and rotted flesh out of his wound and gradually it started to heal.

"There were other cases … there was another soldier with a .45 caliber slug in his jaw and his jaw was puffed up like a balloon. We learned that any foreign object in your body would eventually work its way to the surface. It certainly did in his case, and one day he spit it out. Another soldier had a bullet go through his skull. Believe it or not, it entered one side of his forehead by the temple and came out the other. He showed us the scars on both sides of his head. He was still alive to tell that story.

Hershey

"There was another young fellow who was only fifteen years old. He said he lied about his age to get into the service. He had to have both of his legs amputated because after he was wounded he was caught in the winter months in North Korea where, as I have already said, the temperatures got very, very cold. The word was that the Chinese had allowed some American missionary doctor to do the operation. This young soldier survived that. There's a lot of different cases that are hard to believe that a person could survive anything like that.

"We found out that you had to have the will to live, for one thing, if you wanted to make it back alive. There were many younger soldiers who refused to eat the food that the Chinese gave us to eat on the march up the peninsula. They did not survive to make it to the camp alive.

"About this time, I was just about at the end of my rope ... just before I was ready to give up on the march, I began imagining and seeing things. I don't know why ... but one day, I saw a stack of pancakes as plain as day. They were swimming in syrup and had butter running all over them and I caught myself reaching out for them, thinking I could touch them.

"Shortly after that, we arrived at this camp...not a camp, a village. Every day we had to make so many kilometers and march a certain amount of distance to reach a predesignated place where the guards were changed off, and another group of guards would take over. Consequently, we had that schedule to keep up and we couldn't take our time in marching, it was at a pretty good pace, and you had to keep up. Shortly after I had seen this pancake mirage, we came to this village, and as I said, I was about ready to give up and I thought I could not go on any more.

Hershey

"When we were settled down to rest for the evening, I happened to be seated next to a Korean hooch [n.b. military slang for a hut] where there was a lady … I knew that the Koreans had been under Japanese occupation for many years and that it was compulsory that they all learn to speak and read Japanese. With what little Japanese I had learned from my untraditional upbringing at home, I got it across to her that I was hungry and that I needed food very much. She made me some of what she said she had, which was not rice, but was millet, maybe with a few grains of rice. From that time on, after she had given me that food, I started feeling better and thought I could make it.

"As a result of this encounter, I continued on and I didn't give up. I will always remember that anonymous, caring woman for that simple act of supreme kindness.

"Marching, generally northwards, we continued on for the approximately 30-days that it took us to get to our prisoner-of-war camp. I learned later that it was probably the furthest camp north in North Korea, and another prisoner estimated that it was about 40 miles from the Yalu River and 40 miles from the Yellow Sea. It was called Camp 1. I think it was on the Northwestern part of North Korea, right by the Chinese border. [n.b. camp location listed in documents as Chiangsong or alternatively Ch'ang Ni, North Korea]

"When we arrived at the camp, which was not much different from the villages we had stopped in, they assigned nine of us to a little area which was about a 9x10 foot room. And that was where we were to spend the next 26 months. We slept head and toe, toe and head, on straw mats on a dirt floor. We each had one blanket and no personal toiletries. Every morning, no matter how cold it was, they woke us before daylight and made us go out and cut down trees and bring back the wood. Then, when you got back, you were given one cup of soy milk. That was breakfast.

"We were given a cup, a small bowl, and a brass spoon. The rations did not get much better, but as I said, we were at least given what we were told was soybean milk for breakfast. We also got a bowl of whatever vegetables they had at the time … potatoes, or beets, or turnips, that was for lunch, and for dinner we were given a bowl of either cooked sorghum or millet gruel and that was it. On their Communist holidays we received what, I guess, was white rice soup with a few scraps of meat, usually along with some maggots. This was a *real* treat for us all!" Obviously said with tongue-in-cheek.

Hershey

"Our hut did not have to form-up for exercise since most of us were down with dysentery and were too weak for exercise. Some of us could barely make it to the trench-latrines to relieve ourselves."

Dan L. McKinney, a Camp 1 POW friend of Hershey's, states that Hershey was called "Mike" because no one could pronounce his last name with ease, and no one knew about his nickname of Hershey.

Dan believes that he, himself, was probably the person most instrumental in getting all the latrines closed and moved down to the river and getting all the civilian wells closed. They were the prime cause of the amoebic dysentery [n.b An acute disease caused by ingesting substances contaminated with the amoeba *Entamoeba histolytica* and characterized by severe diarrhea, nausea, and inflammation of the intestines] that killed as many as 25 men a day.

Dan was 24, and most of the other men were young enlistees, seventeen or eighteen years old… it was too easy to go to the well and drink the cold water instead of waiting to boil the water and then taking the time to wait for it to cool. The civilian wells were right next to the latrines before that time.

"I don't know if you're familiar with lice, but when one person has them, you never get rid of them. There's always one person who won't try or improperly cleanses themself, so it was pretty hard to get rid of those lice. They leave scars that stay with you a long time.

"Usually during the afternoon we were pretty much allowed freedom of movement, but only within the confines of the company area. After the first year, we were given some sports equipment … basketballs and baseballs.

"We were eventually allowed to write letters home to our families and I was able to write about a dozen letters home, the last of which was written in January 1952 and was received by my sister Michiko in Los Angeles, California in January of 1953."

Hershey

For three months, Hershey's wife Terry had been telling herself that Hershey couldn't be dead… Then one day Terry went to the post office for the mail and found a tattered brown envelope addressed to her. Instantly she recognized the handwriting as her husband's.

"I started to tremble," she recalls today. "I knew in a flash that Hershey was alive, and at least well enough to write. There were only a few lines saying that he was well and was not being mistreated. I ran back to my father-in-law's restaurant. I must have shouted the news to everyone I passed on the street."

"I never received any of the many packages that I eventually found that my family had sent me. In the last month before my release some men did get some packages finally. I didn't know anyone who got a package before that, if they were sent. Both Michiko and my wife Terry were writing to me at Camp 1.

"There was a central kitchen and each man in the hut had to take his turn picking up the meal … they gave us one bowl per hut. Each member in our hut had to take a turn and go to the kitchen where the food was cooked. The cooks had a big pot and they dished it up into the bowl for each hut. Each member had to take his turn going after the food, and when your turn came up you got your chance to get a little more food because when you ladled out the soup or broth, you naturally gave yourself a little more than you usually got. But that is how we got by as far as rations went.

"When we first arrived, we were interrogated again. Each of us was questioned separately. We sat while they questioned us. Although I heard of beatings of some of the prisoners, I personally was never beaten. Some prisoners would not cooperate at all, and they were put in a cage in the open and had to suffer the harsh weather." [n.b. a related source reported that temperatures that winter were as low as -41°F in the vicinity of this POW camp.]

Hershey

Compare that to Editor Bill Hosokawa, writing for the <u>Denver Post</u>, who relates,

"Sgt. Hershey Miyamura of Gallup, N.M., whose story is on page 12, is the only living Medal of Honor winner of Japanese extraction. Because of his racial origin, he told Empire Editor Bill Hosokawa, he was subjected to especially rough treatment during the 28-months he was a prisoner of the Communists in Korea.

"The Reds kept trying to make him admit he was a Japanese national. Hershey maintained he was a Yank."

"I was captured by Chinese soldiers and throughout my time in POW camp there was nothing but Chinese guards. There were interrogators and interpreters who spoke English who were educated in Russia or in the University in China.

"The first few months we were there, they were trying to brainwash us and convince us that Capitalism was wrong and Communism was right. They told us that we had to read their Communist propaganda pamphlets and books and share our opinions with each other, while an interpreter was there to monitor our talks. This took place in our hut. He would sit in on these 'mandatory' sessions and he would report to the Company Commander as to how we were progressing. But for some reason or another, on our part, we would always convince our interpreter that these documents were outdated and no longer true.

"Most of the materials they were giving us about America were about conditions during the Depression years in the early thirties, and we told them they were outdated and we no longer lived like that these days. But we also had an informer sitting in, we learned later that there were twenty-one informers in the various camps, and the informer in our camp area would report to the Commander about the interpreter believing what we were telling him. We did not know this was going on until the final days of our internment. I guess they realized that they couldn't indoctrinate us into the Communist way of thinking and they gave up on our sessions so we no longer had to attend them.

Hershey

"You went out on wood detail, which we did, to get wood for our cooking fires and to heat our crude shelter in the winter. We had to go out four to five miles to get the wood, cut it up and then haul it all the way back to our shelter."

Again, the following information was revealed in his interview with Editor Bill Hosokawa:

"Not once during his imprisonment was he provided any sort of medical treatment. A leg wound, caused by flying grenade fragments, was never tended. It healed of its own accord in about a year.

"The Chinese gave some G.I.'s pills when they contracted dysentery, which was frequently, but Hershey never was issued any. When his gums became infected and it seemed all of his teeth would fall out, Hershey rubbed salt into the sores and cured himself."

"You always did something to make time pass. Mostly we talked about home and family. Food was the favorite topic since our daily rations were really miserable. I remember some of my hut-mates, George Itagaki, Edward Klimus, Mickey Scott, and Wayne Pickett. I still exchange Christmas cards with them. At Camp 1 in our Company area, I also met Raymond J. McAuliffe. I also met another prisoner, Dan L. McKinney, who I found out was also from New Mexico, Clovis, I think. We became the best of friends, in fact, I eventually named my three children in honor of that friendship and his Irishness."

Dan L. McKinney related that he had never realized this connection about the names of Hershey's children and he was quite moved when he became aware of it. He and Hershey looked after each other when they got sick and each encouraged the other when times were rough. They also discussed buying a restaurant. He thinks that this project was pivotal in giving them a goal that facilitated their getting through each day by giving them something to look forward to, as well as helping them fantasize about the food they would serve in it.

"The unlucky ones had to go out on wood detail, but to get out of going out after wood on these wood details, being that I had dysentery almost all the time I was in the camp and it was freezing cold, I volunteered to be the company barber. I did not know what I was doing when I first started, but I eventually got to be pretty good at it, I think, because the Chinese Company Commander also had his haircut and shave done by me. I was given a pair of scissors, a straight

Hershey

razor, a stropping strap, hand clippers and a comb as equipment. I used an old piece of clothing to put around my 'customers' neck while I was cutting their hair. My compensation for being the barber, as I have already indicated, was that I did not have to trudge out five miles and cut wood on the wood gathering detail.

"As the months passed, our days in camp got a little better. Our captors gave us some better athletic equipment so we could play different sports ... whatever we desired. We usually played catch, boxed some, and played basketball. During a typical day, we played a little, walked around the company area, and sat and talked about what we would do when we got released and got to go home. The topics were mostly centered around food, cooking, and our families.

"Then as the talks and negotiations continued, we got better treatment... That's when they let us start building our own bunk beds. I guess they were three high and we now at least had a little walking space in our hut area. There was no heat in our hut so the winters got pretty cold.

"All we could think about was going home because we kept hearing about the peace talks. But we were also in for a lot of disappointment because the Chinese would always say our side was not willing to cooperate so the peace talks would break down, and we would not hear any more about it for a time. Therefore our emotions were high one time and would drop down in the dumps when the peace talks broke off. It got so we didn't believe anything that anyone was saying. We just took one day at a time."

Hershey

His fellow POW Camp 1 mate, Dan L. McKinney, says that about this time he bet "Mike" $100 that they would be released before the 4th of July in 1953. "Of course," he said, "I lost that bet but Hershey, I know his name now, would not let me pay it off."

"The Chinese soon found out that some of the boys were growing marijuana. I never did know what marijuana smelled like or anything but some of the fellows were getting high and I just didn't know how or why they were getting that way. They were acting awfully strange. Some of the fellows would actually go into convulsions when they first tried it.

"The Chinese Camp Commander soon found out about it and there was a shake-down inspection, and they confiscated it all, whoever was growing it … all the plants, but they did let us keep the pepper plants that we were growing. We used to boil the peppers and then poured the juice over the sorghum or millet, and it made it a little easier to take that way."

Chinese prison Camp 1 Tabasco™ sauce!

"The only time we got rice was during their May Day celebration, which was their big day and they really celebrated it and gave us much better rations just on that particular day. That was the only time we got white rice, as I said.

"We did get 'sweepings' from their tobacco … which was a very mild tobacco. But we did not realize how mild until our final months, when the Chinese and North Koreans began to let people receive letters from home. We knew from the letters that packages being sent to us, some containing cartons of cigarettes, were not getting through the Chinese guards. Some of the letters also contained cigarettes, wrapped in tin-foil within them.

Hershey

"When someone received some cigarettes they would pass one around and then you found how strong our cigarettes were in comparison to theirs. My first drag from one of these cigarettes was so strong it was like getting kicked in the chest from the tobacco. We'd gotten so used to their tobacco. But they never gave us … this was in a sack of loose tobacco, but they never gave us that real cigarette paper. We had to do with just whatever we could get for paper. I always managed to have tobacco because some of the boys didn't smoke and they always gave me their tobacco. Of course, that turned out to be a bad thing for me. I think that is why I have so many problems breathing today."

His friend Dan L. McKinney relates that the prisoners used the <u>Shanghai News</u> [n.b. an English-language Chinese newspaper that was given to the POWs] until they finally managed to

acquire some Chinese rice paper to use for the purpose of cigarette paper.

"After the peace talks finally started progressing, and after they signed the Armistice, they started slowly taking members of our unit out, and we didn't know where they were sending them or anything. They would call out names of prisoners who were going to leave that day. Just small groups at a time. Until our group got so

small, there were only about twenty of us left, and we were the last to be told we were going to leave the camp. We wondered among ourselves if there was some reason why our names had not been called yet. But it was all just a mystery.

"Eventually we were loaded onto a truck and driven to the rail-siding. We boarded the train, if you can call it that; we were loaded into a boxcar, where we were all very somber and quiet. So many rumors had been flying around for so long, we just wanted to see what was going to happen. We were not convinced that we were being released and I guess we were mentally preparing ourselves for some Communist trick."

Hershey

Shades of the Nazi death trains of World War II! I would imagine those thoughts might have flickered through the minds of the other prisoners, as they did through Hershey's.

"Then we arrived at the transfer station and we again traveled the last few miles by truck, and they drove us to Freedom Village at Pan Mun Jom and that is where our tents were set up right across from the North Korean tents.

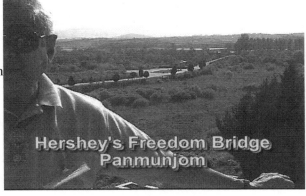

Hershey's Freedom Bridge Panmunjom

"On one side was the American side, and when we saw 'Old Glory' flying, there was not a dry eye in our group. When we crossed over there wasn't a sound made. No one yelled or made a sound because we were still in a state of shock. We didn't actually believe we were really crossing over to our side to freedom. I was released August 21st 1953."

Upon learning the news of his release and homecoming, his wife Terry is quoted as saying, *"It's all so wonderful!"*

Hershey

His sister Michiko, relates,

"*The strangest thing, the way we found out about Hersh being alive and that he was released... we were just visiting home from California in early August, and my Dad said they still haven't found Hersh yet, 'But, he said, He will be coming home.' He never gave up. Because his name had not come out on any list and they didn't know for two years either, he was just 'missing in action' and no one knew anything.*

"*When we came back to California two weeks later, he was released. Our friend Richard Shinto called me at six o'clock in the morning and said, 'Do you know Hersh was just released? The picture of his release was just on television. I said, 'what? From where?' He said he had been a prisoner for over two years. I immediately called the <u>Los Angeles Times</u>, and I said, 'Where did you get the AP photo', because by that time we had gone out and gotten the paper. 'I'm his sister and we've been waiting for over two years to see news about him.' The person at the paper gave me the number of this Major to get a hold of, and when I called him, he told me that Hersh was going to be released and was going to receive the Congressional Medal of Honor.*

"*I said can you get hold of my brother Kei in Northern Japan, because he was in the Air Force there? They did contact the commander and Kei was quite shocked because he was called into the office of the Commanding Officer and he wondered, 'What did I do?' But the commander congratulated my brother on the fact that Hersh was alive and was being released by the North Koreans and was going to be receiving the Medal of Honor. The Air Force said that he was going to be allowed to come home to Gallup, for the reunion. Kei came back and then he received a new assignment and was stationed at March Air Force Base, just outside of Riverside, California.*"

[n.b. He did not make it to Gallup for the reunion, but did meet Hershey in Washington, D.C. for the ceremonies there].

That same newspaper article also had a photograph of three of Hershey's sisters, all in the Los Angeles area, holding a picture of Hershey, and smiling. The photograph was a Mirror Foto. The sisters in the photograph were: Mrs. Shig Sasaki [Shigeko], Mrs. Suzi Tanikawa [Shizuko], and Mrs. Paul Yoshida [Michiko].

Another clipping, related that his sister Michiko was listening to the radio in Los Angeles, California when the news of her brother's release was announced. She called her other Hershey two sisters living in the area, Shizuko, and Shigeko, and they gathered at her home where a later broadcast informed them that Hershey had been wounded on the eve of his capture, but that he was now recovered. In whatever mail that the family had received, there was never mention of his having been wounded.

Hershey

6

"After we had been de-loused and had taken a shower, we were given some bland food and medical care for open sores and other ailments. We had been given clothing, but I was still in my red-and-white striped prisoner pajamas at the time because the Chinese had given them to us 'new' for our release.

"I was told to report to this one building and an officer met me and told me to follow him and I asked him why and he said, 'There is a newspaper fellow from your hometown who wants to get a story from you.'

"I followed him into this building where there was a desk up front and nothing but floodlights of all kinds. Someone, whom I found out later was General Osborne, was standing at the desk, and I was wondering what was going on. That is when he told me … he said … 'Sgt. Miyamura, you are the winner of the Congressional Medal of Honor.'

"This is how I learned that I had been promoted to Sergeant while in captivity."

Hershey

An Associated Press Wirephoto photograph depicts a very skinny Hershey, still dressed in his red-and-white-striped prison clothes, having his hand shaken by Brig. General Ralph Osborne.

An article, by Darrell Garwood, states in part:

A search of Congressional Medal of Honor records for the Korean war showed today that standards are becoming more rigid for the nation's highest military award.

Seventy-one of the 104 men awarded the medal for service in Korea died in the performance of heroic acts. The 33 living winners, can, if they wish, tell stories of almost miraculous escapes from death.

… The primary condition for the medal is that a man has risked his life "above and beyond the call of duty." More often than not, he faced certain or almost certain death.

Experience has shown that opportunities for such sacrifice most often presented themselves in the type of close, rugged ground combat that marked the entire course of the Korean conflict.

"I remember, all I could say was, 'What? I shouldn't be given full credit, there were many others involved.' Then he proceeded to tell me who he was … I saw the 3rd Division patch so I knew he was the Commanding General there. He wanted me to kind of give my point of view of how I won this Medal of Honor. I was not too good of a speaker, and what with all the surprise and all, and all the lights and people looking at me, plus all the mixed emotions that were brought about by being finally free again after such a long time, I didn't say too much, and maybe I did not make a lot of sense about what I did say."

Once again referring to the editorial by Bill Hosokawa:

"Shy and reticent, Hershey speaks little of his feelings when he was liberated and told he had won the Medal of Honor. But a fill-in on that dramatic scene has been provided by Gordon Gammack of the Des Moines Register and Tribune.

Gammack wrote to [Bill Hosokawa]:

"After all the fanfare of his receiving word that he had won the Medal of Honor, Sergeant Miyamura was taken into a private room by a PIO [Public Information Office] captain. Here he broke down a little bit, sobbed, looked up to the captain and said: 'This is a good country — my country.' "

"For my dough it was the quote of Operation Big Switch [n.b. the exchange of Hershey

prisoners with the Communists after agreement of terms at Pan Mun Jom]. *Mac Johnson of the New York Herald Tribune and I were the only ones who happened to get this angle, so it didn't appear in any of the wire service reports.*"

Gammack, who covered the early phases of the Korean War with [Bill] Hosokawa, had returned to Korea to report on the prisoner exchange.

"I was then allowed to send a telegram to my wife, which I did, as follows:

'DEAREST TERRY, NEVER SO HAPPY TO BE AN AMERICAN AS TODAY. YOUR PRAYERS FOR ME HAVE BEEN ANSWERED. AM FEELING OK, GETTING WONDERFUL CARE. DON'T WORRY ABOUT ME. ON MY WAY HOME BY BOAT. LONGING TO SEE YOU AGAIN. BEST WISHES TO ALL AT HOME. HERSH'

Hershey

"We only stayed in Freedom Village for one day and then we were moved to another camp and reunited with other POWs from Camp 1.

"I was given the choice of either flying home or going on the troopship with the boys. As I had told my wife, I decided that the ocean voyage would be a good time to recuperate so I said, 'I will go back by ship.' Which, it turned out, was a very big mistake.

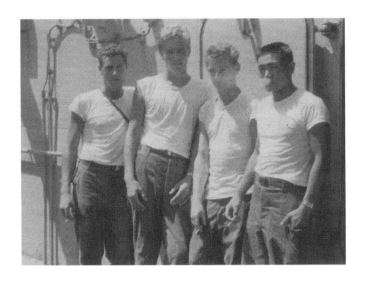

Hershey

"I departed South Korea from the port of Inchon aboard the naval transport ship, USNT Marine Adder.

"We, the released POWs, were in the bottom hold and separated from the other G.I.'s returning to the U.S.

We were interrogated by intelligence agents about the 21 turncoats and informers who had been identified from Camp 1. We also were questioned about how we felt about Communism.

"It took us nineteen days to get back home and I was sick for about eleven of those days. I couldn't get out of that bunk. So, I lost a few more pounds. By the time I got stateside I guess I weighed about 98 pounds."

His reference to his weight here reminded me of the popular Charles Atlas body-building ads that were featured in children's comic books in the 1940s and 1950s, where a burly, tanned brute, with well-defined musculature, was pictured kicking sand in the face of a pale, 98-pound weakling who was lying on the beach, and then walking away arm-in-arm with his very curvaceous girlfriend.

It was obvious that the month-long march up the Korean peninsula and the more than two years in Camp 1 had amputated his sea legs at his lower torso.

While just outside the Golden Gate, on a radio owned by one of the men in the hold, a news broadcast announced that the Medal of Honor winner was aboard and that ceremonies would be conducted dockside and later at a formal dinner that evening. Hershey, ever the shy and reticent guy, asked his fellow POW and good friend, Dan L. McKinney, to accompany him to the ceremonies that evening.

The news report went on to announce that Hershey was going to be flown to Washington, D.C. to receive the Medal of Honor at a special White House presentation by President Dwight D. Eisenhower. Hershey again entreated Dan L. McKinney to accompany him to the ceremony there.

As a measure of the impact that Hiroshi Miyamura's actions had on his fellow Japanese-Americans, here is an excerpt from a newspaper with a Japanese-American audience, sometime in September 1953,

Hershey

" ... During this long imprisonment, Miyamura set an example for his fellow prisoners by vigorously resisting Communist indoctrination. He helped uphold the moral [sic] of his comrades and steeled their will to defy their Red captors. Sergeant Miyamura proved once again that the Communists lie when they charge that America's so-called oppressed minorities are not loyal to the United States. Born of Japanese immigrant parents, Miyamura demonstrated that patriotic Americans can have any color of skin — any racial background."

You may compare those noble and heartfelt feelings with the tact and lack of charm shown by the Army to his wife Terry. She received the following Western Union Telegram from the Army that arrived August 29th 1953 at 7:36 a.m. It read in part, as follows:

> . . . MRS TSURUKU TERRY MIYAMURA=
> GALLUP NMEX=
> THE SECRETARY OF THE ARMY HAS ASKED ME TO
> INFORM YOU THAT YOUR HUSBAND SGT HIROSHI H
> MIYAMURA IS A PASSENGER ABOARD USNT MARINE
> ADDER DUE ARRIVE SAN FRANCISCO PORT OF
> EMBARKATION, FORT MASON, SAN FRANCISCO,
> CALIFORNIA, 5 SEPTEMBER 1953. ARMY WILL DO
> EVERYTHING POSSIBLE TO WELCOME RELATIVES WHO
> ARE IN SAN FRANCISCO TO GREET RETURNING
> SERVICEMEN. HOWEVER, ARMY WILL NOT PROVIDE
> TRANSPORTATION TO SAN FRANCISCO OR MEALS,
> LODGING OR TRANSPORTATION IN SAN FRANCISCO. IF
> YOU PLAN TO MEET SHIP, SUGGEST YOU WIRE OR
> WRITE CG [n.b. Commanding General], SAN FRANCISCO
> PORT OF EMBARKATION AND GIVE NAME OF
> RETURNING SERVICEMAN. UPON YOUR ARRIVAL SAN
> FRANCISCO, DETAILED INFORMATION MAY BE
> OBTAINED FROM CG, SAN FRANCISCO PORT OF
> EMBARKATION, TELEPHONE PROSPECT 6-2200,
> EXTENSION 251=
> WM E BERGIN MAJOR GENERAL USA THE ADJUTANT
> GENERAL OF THE ARMY=

"I was one of 367 repatriated POWs from Korea, plus there were another 1,500 Armed Forces personnel who were returning to the U.S. on rotation from the Orient aboard that troopship.

"They arranged it so that I was the first one off the ship when we finally arrived in San Hershey

Francisco Bay. Terry was there, right by the gangplank, waiting for me. On the pier there were officers, a band, and all the families there to meet us."

Hershey was quoted by the press as saying:

"I am happy and glad to be back. This is the most wonderful country in the world. I am very proud to [have received] the Medal. It is a wonderful honor."

"[Sgt. Miyamura] was greeted by Lt. Gen. Joseph M. Swing, Commanding General, 6th Army, from the Presidio, San Francisco, and Brig. Gen. James M. Lewis, Commanding General, of Camp Stoneman, located in the San Francisco Bay Area, who both lifted a salute to pay tribute to Sgt. Miyamura, the 62nd Medal of Honor winner from the Korean war, in the time honored fashion. Hershey returned their salute, then embraced his wife Terry, who was crying openly, with a hero-type hug and a kiss that lasted fully two minutes, while newsreel and news photographers recorded the joyous meeting."

"I was assigned an NCO, Sgt. L. Stevens, of Seattle, as an aide during my stay in San Francisco. Sgt. Stevens was a member of the Sixth Army Guard of Honor and a veteran himself of fifteen months in Korea."

During the festivities of the arrival of the troop transport, Terry was quoted as saying:

"This is the happiest day of my life; happier even than our wedding day."

There were 16 members of Hershey's family there to greet him upon his arrival, ranging in age from his 2_-year old nephews, Alan and Ronnie, to his 65-year old father, Yaichi.

Hershey

"Our whole family was booked into the posh St. Francis Hotel in downtown San Francisco on Union Square, as guests of the San Francisco Chapter of the Japanese-American Citizens League [JACL]."

Terry and Hershey were honored at a private reception at the Marines' Memorial Club that evening, that was hosted by the National and San Francisco chapters of the JACL, the Townsend Harris American Legion Post No. 438, and the Golden Gate Nisei Memorial Post of the VFW 9879.

Hershey is reported by the press, after acknowledging a standing ovation, of making this brief statement to the gathered guests:

"Very happy to be back. I'm glad to be an American. I want to thank every one of you."

The article went on to say:

"The modest sergeant's short speech typifies his personality. It is difficult to place him as the same man who single-handedly wiped out more than 50 enemy troops while defending a machine-gun position and while protecting the retreat of his fellow soldiers."

Hershey also received four special citations and other tokens of appreciation at the reception.

"Also honored at the same event was my friend, Dan L. McKinney, who was held prisoner in the same company with me at Camp 1. He had agreed to accompany me earlier that day outside the Golden Gate, while still aboard the Marine Adder.

"While I was traveling home from San Francisco after being released from North Korea, I was holding forth with songs that I had learned in the prisoner-of-war camp."

Reportedly, these were not always in the best of taste and were often ribald, as is the custom of servicemen, much to the chagrin of his family.

Hershey

During a family interview, his sister, Michiko, maintained that Hersh is a good singer with a very good voice, although there was some good natured dissension among other family members about this. His sister, Shizuko, says that as children Hershey and Michiko would stand in front of a mirror singing to see who was the best singer.

Another sister, Momoko, also in Hershey's defense, relates that Hersh, one time, at a monthly dance held in cooperation with the Japanese-Americans from Albuquerque, N.M., answered a challenge and got up and sang "Sunday, Monday or Always." [n.b. an old Bing Crosby tune that was released in 1943 and was a million seller, as well as topping the Billboard charts for seven weeks] She avows that Hershey did it quite well, was applauded by the dancers, and had a very nice voice.

"Terry and I went to East Los Angeles because her mother lived there and shortly, after a few days, we were getting ready to return to Gallup and I received a phone call and I was asked to delay my return trip for a day or two. I couldn't figure out why, but I said O.K.

"Terry and I departed Los Angeles on Santa Fe's Super Chief and, I learned later, with the help of the Army, the railroad was induced into making a special 'whistle-stop' in Gallup, where the super-liner did not normally make a stop for passengers."

Members of his family, including his father, his wife's mother, and his brother Kei's wife, had departed the West Coast a day earlier and formed a three-car caravan to Gallup. They wanted to arrive in time for the ceremonies planned for the hero's return to his hometown.

Hershey

As he awaited the arrival of his son and daughter-in-law at the train station, Hershey's father, Yaichi Miyamura, was quoted as saying:

"Everything … everything is okay now."

"Well, then we finally did arrive home. When we entered Gallup by train, all I could see was an immense crowd of people there."

The mayor of Gallup had declared September 9th as "Hiroshi Miyamura Day."

There were almost 4,000 people crowding the station platform for about a 100 yards and spilling over into Santa Fe Plaza, to greet the returning hometown hero. Another source places the number at nearer 5,000, and subsequent writeups tout that there were almost 10,000 attendees at the welcoming celebration, which would mean that somewhere between half and almost all of the residents of the city of Gallup had joined the celebration at track-side. What a grand statement of civic pride!

Mikoyan-Gurevich MiG-15 "Fagot"
USAF Museum

They had even closed the schools for a half-day. Additionally, almost all of the merchants in town closed their businesses until noon to allow their employees an opportunity to join in the festivities.

Hershey

Momentary confusion was caused as Hershey stepped down from the train because his burnished-aluminum coach car had passed beyond the group of waiting dignitaries, honor guard, and members of his family before coming to a complete stop, but Hershey trotted back to join them, so that the ceremonies could commence.

North American F-86A "Sabre"
USAF Museum

Hershey's arrival was signaled by a flight of four F-86 Sabre jets [n.b. the famed Mig-15 killers in the Korean War that had attained a phenomenal combat record of 792 kills vs. 76 losses] that screamed over the delighted crowd in four high-speed, low-altitude, tree-top formation passes in tribute to the Medal of Honor winner.

Hershey and his wife Terry, who was holding a large bouquet of white carnations, were met by New Mexico's Senator Guido Zecca and Col. John P. MacFarland, a representative of the Governor of New Mexico and were escorted through an Air Force Honor Guard who formed an open corridor from the station platform to the speaker's stage.

The VFW drum and bugle corps and the Gallup Municipal band played martial music to the accompaniment of the cheering throng of well wishers. The colors were presented by the Farmington, New Mexico, VFW Color Guard and other VFW units who had brought their honor guards too, and there was a welcoming committee who included Senator Zecca and the representative of the Governor of New Mexico, both with expressions of New Mexico's and Gallup's pride in Hershey and their joy at his safe return.

Hershey

The speaker's stand had a large white banner behind it with, **"Hi Hershey Welcome Home to Gallup**," painted on it.

According to a clipping from The <u>Gallup Independent,</u> as Hershey mounted to the speaker's stand, his childhood friend and comrade in arms through World War II, Amelio DiGregorio, broke down and tearfully embraced him.

Hershey was then presented with an honorary colonel's commission on the governor's staff by the Governor's representative, Col. John P. MacFarland. The Mayor of Gallup, "Mickey" Mollica, then welcomed Hershey back to town and a thunderous cheer was raised when the Mayor introduced Terry, who had already been presented with a large floral arrangement of carnations, and Mr. Yaichi Miyamura to the crowd.

The National Director of the Japanese-American Citizens League, Masao Satow, then welcomed Hershey back home. This was followed

by a speech by Charles Hunt, the local VFW commander, who made a presentation to Hershey of a Life Membership in the VFW.

Hershey

The commander of the local American Legion, James Tadlock, and A.L. Wood, Jr., the state commander of the VFW, also expressed the good wishes of all their respective veteran members. Charles Matsubara of the JACL was also present with other members of the Albuquerque chapter of the JACL who had raced westward in a motorcade to greet one of their members, the hometown hero. Even Judy Stewart with the local Girl Scout troop presented Hershey with a gift and a welcome home.

Then the surprised hometown hero was presented a check by his long time friend, Amelio DiGregorio, for $3,850 that had been collected for the "Miyamura Gift Fund." This was a result of a <u>Gallup Independent</u> newspaper campaign subsequent to learning of Hershey's release from the POW camp and his award of the Congressional Medal of Honor three weeks earlier.

Hershey then thanked the well wishers, *"Words cannot express my thoughts now, but it's good to be home in Gallup."* Any further words were unnecessary as the jubilant crowd again broke into sustained cheering and shouting as they demonstrated their understanding of a hero's joy at being home among friends and neighbors.

For such a shy and reticent hero, it must have been quite an occasion for Hershey, along with his father and his wife, who were seated on the speaker's platform during the entire ceremony and with the rest of the Miyamura clan surrounding the speaker's stand.

Then there was a break in the ceremonies while photographers and newsmen from the wire services and newspapers throughout the Western U.S. took even more photos and conducted hurried interviews for their respective papers. Meanwhile the crowd was breaking up and heading for Route 66, Gallup's main street, for a parade from the train station, thence to First and Second Avenues, terminating a block from Hershey and Terry's home.

Hershey

"   That was quite a welcoming home. We got into a convertible driven by my cousin, Frank Uyeda, with my father in the front seat and Terry and I in the back seat. Then I was told to get up on the back of the seat, and we drove from the train station to our house, along the route of all these cheering people who wanted to reach out and shake my hand. At that time we lived quite a little ways from the station."

The route of the parade was thronged by well-wishers, veterans, school children, and friends. The cavalcade was preceded by a Gallup police car and fire engine, both with their emergency flashers pulsing and their sirens ululating like a pair of banshees in heat.

Then followed the American Legion color guard, unfortunately photographically memorialized for all time, marching out of step.
Then came the VFW Drum and Bugle corps preceded by a lovely majorette, twirling her baton and strutting her stuff.

Behind them followed an Honor Guard formed by 38 non-commissioned officer members of the Air Force's Continental Divide early-warning radar facility. In several cars following Hershey were the other members of his family, the Senator, Governor's representative, Mayor, and representatives from the Army and the Air Force. Then came marching groups from the Boy Scouts, Girl Scouts, Cub Scouts, and Brownies.

Hershey

This was followed by an assemblage composed of the membership of other veteran and civic organizations present at the ceremonies. Finally, as the parade passed by them, the townspeople enthusiastically joined in the parade.

There was a dinner dance given that evening in Hershey's honor, at the Gallup Country Club.

According to a newspaper article, probably from the <u>Gallup Independent,</u> bylined by Hank Stern:

"Sgt. Hiroshi Miyamura was welcomed home to his family and his people last night at a reception and dinner given him by the JACL at the Country Club.

"About 100 people, mostly Japanese-Americans, were present to shout, 'Welcome, Hershey, welcome.' as the Medal of Honor winner, his wife and father came through the door.

" 'There are only about 18 members of the JACL here in Gallup,' said Mrs. Ann Shibata, who helped arrange the celebration, 'and we've stuck pretty close together, somewhat like a big family.'

"And it was a family party last night. Some of the men and women helped to prepare the buffet dinner, slicing up heaping platters of ham and turkey and putting them out for the guests. Only a handful of outsiders were present. The rest were old friends. ...

"... The sergeant and his wife came into the room and then went up and down the buffet line greeting family and friends from Gallup, Albuquerque, and all over the West, who had come to the celebration. ... "

Hershey

"I was trying to become used to being back home and having real American home-cooked food and no one watching you all the time.

"So much happened in my life after that."

A sampling of the family scrapbooks provides an insight into the events surrounding that simple statement.

Around this time, the Honorable Edwin L. Mechem, Governor of New Mexico referred to Hershey as New Mexico's most outstanding citizen. He said, "*Sgt. Hiroshi Miyamura represents the finest qualities of American manhood. His heroic action in our fight against the tyranny of totalitarian ideology will live in history as an example of highest courage and greatest devotion. Freedom-loving people everywhere will forever be indebted to Hiroshi Miyamura, New Mexico's most outstanding citizen.*"

He and Terry were invited back to Los Angeles in September, 1953, by 20th Century Fox for the premiere of "*The Robe,*" and by several Nisei veteran organizations for a banquet in Hershey's honor the following evening.

According to separate items in the Crossroads, The Los Angeles Nisei Weekly and The Rafu Shimpo, the co-sponsoring organizations were: the Nisei Veterans Coordinating Council, (which was partially made up of: Commodore Perry Post 525 of the American Legion; VFW, Nisei Memorial Post 9938; VFW, Gardena, 4th District Nisei Memorial, Post 1961; Disabled American Veterans Nisei Chapter [100]; and the Nisei Veterans Association), JACL, and the Japanese Chamber of Commerce of Southern California.

Hershey

The 20th Century Fox publicity staff took Hershey and his wife for an escorted tour of the studio, rubbing elbows with some movie stars, and then to lunch at the Hollywood Roosevelt Hotel. They were then escorted to Grauman's Chinese Theater for the world premier of "*The Robe*," in CinemaScope™ and Technicolor™.

According to Cobina Wright, in her column, *Society as I Find It*, in the <u>Los Angeles Times</u>:

> "*Everyone's getting their diamonds and minks ready for the tremendous Hollywood premiere of Lloyd C. Douglas' "<u>The Robe</u>" … Practically every celebrity in town is scheduled to be there – it should be one of the most brilliant premiers ever to shake Hollywood. … An equally brilliant after-premiere supper dance is being planned at Romanoff's in the Crown Room.*"

The next day, September 25th, Hershey, Terry, and other family members were present at the previously heralded , "Sgt. Hiroshi Miyamura Testimonial Banquet," in the Pacific Room at the Statler Hotel. Hershey was presented a plaque on behalf of the sponsoring civic and veterans groups. These included the Nisei Veteran's Coordinating Council, Japanese-American Citizen's League, and the Japanese Chamber of Commerce of Los Angeles.

The dinner was highlighted by "Roast Native Duckling with Apple Sauce," as noted on the souvenir menu that was kept by Hershey's sister Michiko, and her husband, Paul Yoshida. The principal speaker was Maj. General Hobart R. Gay, III, former Commanding General of the 1st Cavalry Division in Korea, who said in part:

> "*You are a credit to your country. … And in the battlefield, Sgt. Miyamura's courage, and the desire to do what is right resulted in his winning the country's highest award. And his great deed makes him a hero in the world's exclusive fraternity: the brotherhood of the fighting men. General Patton, Jr. once said he would rather win a Congressional Medal of Honor than become president of the United States. Your country is proud to pay you homage tonight. I salute you with humility. God bless you!*"

Hershey then responded; "*I wish I can express how happy I am tonight. To you who have made this grand party possible, and a great success, I want to thank you. I am deeply honored.*"

Hershey

On September 26th, the day after the banquet, another clipping reveals that MGM Studios, not to be outdone by 20th Century Fox, arranged a private screening of "<u>Go For Broke</u>," the MGM movie about the famed Japanese-American 442nd RCT. This is the same unit that Hershey served in during the end of World War II.

Because Hershey was in a POW camp in 1951 when it was released, he had never gotten to see it. This was in the days before VCRs! The article went on:

"Before the screening, we had lunch at the studio commissary as MGM guests. Terry, his wife, obviously was more thrilled at seeing such stars as Stewart Granger, Howard Keel, Vittorio Gassman

[and others] … [they] were given a treat when Mr. Herty [of MGM publicity] arranged their visit to Studio 23 where they were shooting the Technicolor[TM] production 'Rose Marie.' After watching the shooting of several scenes, [Hershey's] party had pictures taken with the two stars, Howard Keel, in the bright red uniform of the Royal Northwest

Mounted Police, and little Ann Blyth, who in her moccasins [buckskin outfit and sporting a fur hat] proved to be shorter than the Nisei girls. Small, but m-m-m! Hersh was feted at a reunion of his 442nd buddies at the home of Kaz Inouye on [September 29th]."

Driving back toward Gallup a few days later, on October 3rd, according to another clipping, this one from a Phoenix, Arizona newspaper, the Miyamura's stopped off as the invited guests of the American Legion Post 29 of Glendale, Arizona. Here, Hershey was made an Honorary Citizen of Arizona in a presentation by Arizona's Attorney General, Ross Jones, acting for Arizona's Governor Howard Pyle.

Hershey

In the same article, Hershey, with regard to the heavy indoctrination procedures the prisoners were subjected to by the Communists in Camp 1, quipped, *"But we only studied when the guards were watching."*

"I was not used to getting attention like this. Crowds, applause, and people handing me plaques, certificates, and keys to the city. I mean, wasn't I the quiet lad from Gallup, New Mexico, for crying out loud?

"I got a notice to report to Ft. Bliss, Texas, near the city of El Paso, I believe it was in the early part of October, for my discharge, [n.b. Hershey was discharged on October 9, 1953] and I was told I could bring any friends or relatives that I wanted. I had my wife, father, and my cousin Frank, the auto mechanic, accompany me to Texas. My friend, Dan L. McKinney also accompanied us and was discharged in a separate ceremony. He was joined by his father, S.J. McKinney.

"The reason for that was the commander there, [n.b. Major General S.B. Mickelson], had planned a parade and all the troops passed in review while I was standing there on the stand with the General, so that was quite an honor. Then we spent a day or two there at the fort."

Hershey

Dan L. McKinney relates that it was at this time that he was artfully able to retire the debt that he owed Hershey from their bet made during their time in prison camp. While shopping in Ciudad Juarez, a Mexican border town near El Paso, Hersh's wife Terry saw some alligator shoes that she really ached for, but they just cost too much. Dan, seizing upon the opportunity, bought her the shoes and a matching purse, and thus he satisfied his debt of honor.

In a newspaper clipping, possibly from the <u>Gallup Independent</u>, datelined Gallup, New Mexico:

"… [Hershey] and his wife, formerly of Winslow, Arizona, were honored by the El Paso American Legion post during a convention in Texas, and also were guests of the Las Cruces' Veterans of Foreign Wars group in New Mexico on their return trip [from Ft. Bliss, Texas]."

Hershey

Hershey was quoted as saying [referring to his discharge at Ft. Bliss, Texas], *"They offered me a commission in the Army ... but I'd be satisfied as a staff sergeant if I did rejoin. I've got 90-days to think it over, and if this restaurant deal falls through,* [n.b. He was looking into a business venture with Dan L. McKinney] *I may re-enlist. I don't know right now."*

"Shortly after that I got the notice to report to the White House and again I was told you could bring a friend or relatives with you. For this reason my brother, Kei, who was a sergeant in the Air Force at Misawa Air Base, in Northern Japan, at the time, got flown back to stateside."

Kei flew to Washington, where he was joined by his wife Kimi, Hershey's wife and father, Dan L. McKinney and his wife Joyce Ann, and Hershey's hometown best friend, Amelio DiGregorio and his wife Ann Jean.

His sister Michiko, the de facto family historian, says that this limited selection of family members was because of the Japanese tradition of not being a burden when a guest of someone. The family members decided that only Hershey and his wife Terry, his father, his brother Kei and his wife, would be the ones who would go and get to spend the offered week in Washington to see the ceremony as guests of Uncle Sam.

His brother Kei had a comment to add about this time. He had been flown back from his base in Northern Japan to Hamilton Air Base, just north of San Francisco, and he did not know that his wife had also been contacted by a service representative and was going to go to Washington D.C., too. "I had received about $600.00 in travel pay to get a plane ticket and I thought, 'Man, if I take a slow train over there, I will save a couple of hundred bucks.' Then I found out my wife Kimi was flying to Washington, so I had to buy a plane ticket that cost about $600.00 to fly out and join her. I saw that money just fly away!"

In an October 23rd 1953 issue of Pacific Citizen, Los Angeles Chapter of the JACL, dateline Washington, D.C., it was noted that Hershey and his party would arrive in Washington, D.C., where he was going to be presented the Medal of Honor by President Eisenhower, in time for ceremonies at Arlington National Cemetery celebrating the annual Nisei Memorial Day services.

Hershey

A photograph, courtesy of <u>Shin Nisei Bei</u>, depicts Hershey placing a wreath at the tombstone of fellow Nisei Pvt. First Class Saburo Tanamachi, a member of the 442nd RCT and one of the first Nisei World War II veterans to be buried at the national cemetery.

The article continues,

> *"Monday noon [October 26th] Eikichi Araki, Ambassador Extraordinary and Plenipotentiary, will honor the Nisei war hero and his party at a luncheon at the Embassy of Japan."*

Hershey

7

"My wife Terry and I were flown from Gallup, via Denver, to Washington, D.C. We were arriving two days in advance of the planned ceremony at the White House to allow time for me to acquire a new uniform. Since with all of the weight that I had lost, I had none that would fit me any longer.

"We were both excited and somewhat unnerved by the upcoming ceremony in Washington, D.C.

"We were met at the airport by the military liaison and a staff car with a driver that would be placed at our disposal during the week-long stay."

Hershey and Terry were guests of the government at the famed Willard Hotel in Washington, D.C., renown as the, "The Resident of Presidents."

Ideally located only one block from the White House, every American President since Zachary Taylor has spent some time at the Willard, many while awaiting inauguration. Franklin Pierce was the first to give the hotel its moniker "the residence of presidents," after a stay at the Willard in 1853. Abraham Lincoln stayed at the Willard while awaiting inauguration, once being smuggled in under cover of darkness because of a rumored assassination attempt. Other notable happenings included, Boston's Julia Ward Howe penning the "Battle Hymn of the Republic" in one of the Willard's rooms after being awakened by marching soldiers, and Martin Luther King, Jr. wrote his "I Have A Dream" speech while staying there in 1968.

Hershey

"I could not get to sleep that night in the Willard. I was so nervous and worried about the ceremony scheduled for the next day, even though the protocol staff had briefed us all on how it would be conducted. I mean, I would be face-to-face with Dwight David Eisenhower, President of the United States of America!

"I awoke in the Willard without having a memory of getting into bed and falling asleep. This was going to be one of the most traumatic days of my life, including even, the night and day of the battle that garnered me the Medal of Honor…

"On October 27th 1953, President Eisenhower presented me with the Congressional Medal of Honor. He asked me… well I can't remember really what he asked me. All I remember is him saying, 'I am very proud to present you this medal.' He shook my hand. I just cannot remember much after that."

His memories here are augmented by those of Joyce Ann McKinney, wife of his good friend Dan, also present who, along with Amelio DiGregorio and his wife Anna Jean, had come to share the occasion with Hershey. She says that Hershey was shaking so bad when President Eisenhower placed the Medal around his neck, that Ike steadied him and said something to the effect, "Relax, Hersh, I'm not going to bite you."

Hershey

Additionally, when the receiving line was moving past to be introduced to President Eisenhower, it was proceeding along with some regularity until it finally ground to a halt. When Joyce Ann looked to see the reason, she saw that Hershey's wife, Terry, was giving the

President a recipe for something or other. President Eisenhower was quite interested in getting all the details she was offering and had an aide jot down the particulars.

His brother Kei with his wife Kimi, part of the family group that joined Hershey in Washington, said about their stay in Washington and the ceremonies at the White House: "We will never have another experience like that. We had two Corporals assigned to us and two cars for our family, and we had a Lieutenant, I think his last name was Rogers, who arranged dinners and shows for us. He took us to lunch at Mount Vernon one day. He took us to a large hotel and we got to see an ice show that, I think, starred Sonja Henie. He also took us on a special tour of the U.S. Mint. Additionally, we were the honored guests of the Japanese Embassy for a very nice lunch."

Family members relate, regarding the presentation ceremony at the White House, "It was very impressive; Hershey was the first one called up. He walked up there and saluted the President and President Eisenhower saluted him back and then presented him with the Medal of Honor and then salutes were exchanged again. All of the pomp and ceremony was very moving and powerful to witness first-hand."

Hershey

Kei's wife, Kimi, went on to say, "I remember finally getting a chance to dance with Hersh at one of the receptions, either in Washington, D.C. or New York, and I really got a chance to speak with him. I did meet him when he had his homecoming in New Mexico, but there were too many other people vying for his attention at that time, and we did not get to spend much time talking. While we were dancing, that is when I got to know him better. He said he had heard we had gotten married and told me that Kei was his little brother."

Numerous newspaper clippings reported that Hershey was the first of seven recipients receiving the nation's highest accolade for military gallantry. They also related that President Eisenhower told Hershey and six other "Korean War" recipients of the Medal of Honor, *"Any man who wins the nation's highest decoration is marked for leadership. And now instead of leading at battle, they must lead toward peace. They must make certain that no other young men follow them up these steps to receive the Medal of Honor."*

Hershey along with two others from the Army and four members of the U.S. Marines were those honored at the ceremony. These seven, according to a newspaper clipping datelined Washington, D.C.:

> *"… were among the largest group of Medal of Honors decorated by Mr. Eisenhower [former five-star general] since he entered the White House."*

Dateline Washington, D.C. (AP):

> *The ceremony took place on the North Portico of the White House, the executive mansion's 'front porch.' … flanking the President as he made the presentations were Secretary of Defense Wilson, civilian and military chiefs of the fighting services and friends and relatives of the men honored. The U.S. Army band played martial airs on the lawn before and after the presentations and an honor guard composed of Marine Corps and Army units presented arms as the President appeared. The President said the gathering symbolized the gratitude of America to the seven young men."*

Hershey

Another clipping relates:

"Niseidom's finest hour in 1953—possibly in all history—came at noon, October 27, on the North Portico of the White House in Washington, D.C., when the President himself personally decorated Sgt. Hiroshi H. Miyamura with the Congressional Medal of Honor.

"First of seven Korean war heroes to be awarded the nation's highest accolade for military gallantry that day, all America thrilled to his epic deeds that have seldom, if ever been surpassed by any American soldier in any war in which the nation has participated since 1776.

"By his actions in the far-off battlefields of Korea, he reminded the world again that, in the words of the late President Franklin D. Roosevelt, 'Americanism is a matter of the mind and heart; Americanism never was, and never will be, a matter of race or ancestry.'

"His deeds recalled for many Americans the 'Go For Broke' spirit of the 442nd RCT [n.b. composed of all Japanese-Americans in World War II, with the exception of the officers] *that earned for itself a record as one of America's all-time finest combat organizations in Italy and France.*

"... The publicity that has been given Hiroshi Miyamura throughout the land has resulted in improving the ever-improving climate of acceptance towards persons of Japanese ancestry.

"This climate of acceptance makes it that much easier for every Issei, Nisei, and Sansei [n.b. first-, second-, and third-generation children of immigrant parents] *to walk the streets in dignity, to look for and to keep jobs for which they are qualified by training and ability, to live decently and to be welcomed by their neighbors wherever they may be.*

Hershey

"In these and many other ways, Hiroshi Miyamura has contributed to the lives and welfare of every person o
Japanese ancestry in this country. Every one of us should be grateful to him for what he has done for us, for the things that he has won for all of us are the intangibles of goodwill that in the long run will help make us 'better Americans in a greater America.' Wherever he has gone, Hiroshi Miyamura has expressed the hope that he will remain a credit to persons of Japanese ancestry. We need to have no fear on that account, for he symbolizes the Medal of Honor in his speech, his actions, and his attitudes.

"It seems to us, rather, that we persons of Japanese ancestry should strive to be a credit to him, for by winning the nation's highest award he has demonstrated anew that there is nothing that we cannot achieve in these United States if we dare to work and fight for it. If there is any tribute that we can pay to our only living Medal of Honor winner, it is by emulating his example of meeting every challenge with courage and faith, knowing that in fighting one's best one will always win a medal of honor."

"We did have a week to see the Capitol. I had a car and a driver and a personal tour guide, a Second Lieutenant. He said, 'You can do whatever you want to do for this week. I will take you wherever you want to go and to whatever you want to see.' I still regret not inviting the rest of my sisters because I didn't know that I could bring my whole family. I thought just a few members could go. Anyway, we enjoyed a week sightseeing at all the historical sights in Washington, D.C. That was quite a memorable visit, too. I think every American should go to Washington to see all those monuments."

Hershey

8

"There had been so many speeches, so many celebrations, certificates, awards, and honors, I never have gotten used to standing in front of an audience and speaking to them. After our return to New Mexico, things were different...

"My father became ill with cancer in 1960, and turned the operation and ownership of the Lucky Lunch Café over to my eldest sister, Chiyo. He moved to California where he could receive care from my sister Michiko and my brother Kei.

"Chiyo ran the business until she was forced to relocate because of a new highway going in. She moved to a location at 66th and First, and named the business, the Liberty Café.

"My father passed away in Los Angeles, in December, 1965. His remains were returned by train from Los Angeles to Gallup, and he was buried beside my mother, Tori."

The children note that their father kept a daily diary as long as he lived, which mysteriously to date, not one of the volumes has turned up among the family belongings.

Hershey

"We came back to Gallup and I applied for a job at the Army Ordinance Depot at Fort Wingate, outside of Gallup. I took the exam and all and I waited, and waited, and didn't hear any word from them. In the meantime there was this fellow who was opening up a new auto-accessory outlet [n.b. he was Frank Rutar], called White Auto Store, similar to the Western Auto chain. It sold the same type of merchandise and he asked me to come and work for him while I was waiting. So I agreed to do that. I needed a change… I didn't want to go back into auto mechanics if I could help it.

"Somehow or other, years went by, and Terry and I had three kids, Mike born in August 1954 [n.b. in another of those quirks of fate, he was born one year to the day after Hershey was released from the prison camp, August 21, 1954], Pat in July 1955, and Kelly in November 1959, which were all named after my Irish friend that I met in prison camp. [n.b. Dan L. McKinney]

"Oh, I finally got the notice from the depot to come and work… and I told them to forget it. By that time I wasn't interested.

"Then seven years went by and in that time, here came this sergeant who was in my same section in Korea, the one whom I had tried to help, who was wounded in the buttocks and had to be left on the road. His name was Joseph Annello. I didn't think I would ever see him again, but here he comes walking through the door. I couldn't believe it. He said about ten days later, our own troops came by and picked them up. Another P.O.W. who was able to walk out got back to our troops to report the location of ten other wounded soldiers that were surviving without food. I don't know why we didn't get to spend any more time than we did but… to this day we keep in correspondence… because now he is not too far from here. He originally was from Boston, Massachusetts but now he's working in Denver, Colorado. We keep in correspondence and he is going to retire in couple of years. He was much younger than I was…he was only seventeen or eighteen at that time and I was 24. I was one of the oldest men there. I did just see him again at the 50th year Korean War Veteran reunion in Las Vegas after our last trip to Korea."

During those intervening seven years, Hershey was a participant in many other functions, some of which are noted here:

The United States Junior Chamber of Commerce, with Headquarters in Tulsa, Oklahoma, announced that Hershey was one of Ten Outstanding Young Men of 1953. He had been nominated, according to the Pacific Citizen, by Senator Guido Zecca and Edwin L. Mechem the Governor of New Mexico added his endorsement.

Hershey

"The ten men, all between the ages of 21 and 36, were chosen for the honor by a board of nationally known judges in an annual selection sponsored since 1938 by the United States Junior Chamber of Commerce."

The article went on to say that the recipients would be honored at a $15-a-plate banquet in their honor in Seattle, Washington on January 23rd 1954.

A clipping relates:

"… In a telegram from Washington, D.C., Senator [Dennis] Chavez [N.M.] commented: 'New Mexico feels most proud of Sgt. Miyamura and very thankful for the recognition given this worthy New Mexico boy [n.b. this racial slur was still being used openly in polite society, back in 1954]. *The Congressional Medal is the recognition of a nation for service far beyond the call of duty."*

In a letter to <u>The Northwest Times,</u> Senator [Clinton P.] Anderson [N.M.] said:

"The Citizens of New Mexico are proud of this splendid soldier who took part in two different wars prior to his capture by the Communists on April 25, 1951. The record of his unusual bravery and remarkable gallantry has not only been recognized by the Government of the United States, but has become one of the treasured possessions of all the people of New Mexico. As a squad leader he protected his men. He did not hesitate to enter into hand to hand combat with the enemy, nor did he fail to make the greatest possible use of his weapons or ammunitions [sic] when they were available to him.

'The people of New Mexico have welcomed him home following his release by the Communists and have been happy to honor him on many public occasions. He is a fine example of the young citizenry of this State which distinguishes itself in time of need regardless of racial origin.

'As a representative of the people of New Mexico I thank you for your courtesy to our citizen and praise you for giving attention to this distinguished Japanese American soldier whose service to his country was truly outstanding,' "

Hershey

Another article noted:

> "*A Medal of Honor winner and 250 new citizens were honored with simple sincere words [on January 22nd, 1954] by the Seattle Japanese American community. A deep loyalty to America and its cherished freedom marked the program throughout.*

> "*... But the couple who won the hearts of the 450 gathered at the Chamber of Commerce auditorium was ex-Sgt. Hiroshi Miyamura, Medal of Honor winner, and his wife, Terry. Mayor Allan Pomeroy presented [Hershey] with a symbolic key to the city. The JACL chapter [in the form of retiring President Dr. Kelly Yamada] gave the Korean war hero a huge [engraved] silver platter.*

> "*... In a Sunday ceremony sponsored by the Nisei Veterans Committee, [Hershey] paid homage by laying a wreath to the Seattle and King County war dead at Memorial Plaza. Later he placed another wreath in tribute to the Nisei war dead at Lakeview Cemetery.*"

On Saturday, January 23rd, 1954, Hershey was honored at the previously announced United States Junior Chamber of Commerce presentation of the "Ten Outstanding Young Men" of 1953, which was held in Seattle, Washington, at the Civic auditorium with a reception at the New Washington Hotel.

An article went on to say that Hershey was the guest of honor at a banquet given by the Utah Junior Chamber of Commerce on February 21st 1954. During the evening of that same day Hershey was the guest of "Mt. Olympus and Salt Lake Clers, [JACL] in an evening at the Pagoda." Hershey said of Salt Lake City, "*I had always wanted to see the city.*" Taciturn, yes, as is his nature.

Hershey

The caption under a photograph contained the following, "*Twenty Two Chicago organizations joined to honor Medal of Honor winner, Sgt. Hiroshi Miyamura at the Morrison Hotel, April 15 [1954] _ another in the succession of awards to the modest and valiant hero of the Korean War.*" Representing Chicago Mayor Kennelly was Joseph McCarthy [not the notorious Wisconsin Senator, the caption warns].

At some time in 1954, Hershey was awarded and named by the JACL as the "Nisei of the Biennium."

In Denver, Colorado on November 29, 1954, during the four day convention of the JACL, Hershey was honored by a standing ovation from the 300 gathered JACL Mountain-Plains District conventioneers. Hershey was named to serve as vice-chairman of the District Council which covers the New Mexico area where Hershey resides. The attendees and Hershey received plaudits from Congressman Byron G. Rogers of Denver (D-Colo.), Lt. Governor of Colorado, Gordon Allott, and other distinguished guests. As usual Hershey, responded without a long-winded speech: "*I wish to thank you and express my appreciation to all of you here. I only hope that in the future I will be a credit to my people.*"

Hershey

9

Night had drawn its curtain of darkness over Gallup and Hershey looked up at the brilliant display of stars in the sky. It always moved him to see this New Mexican panorama of inky darkness punctuated by the splendor of the firmament above. In all of his travels over the years, he had never found its master. The bright band of billions of stars that make up the Milky Way were especially prominent this spring evening.

Hershey got up to move inside, stopping to refill his drink from the container in the refrigerator. He walked into the living room and setting down his glass, he dropped into his favorite easy chair. His thoughts about the past were powerful, although some of the details now eluded his mental grasp. With a deep sigh he closed his eyes and began a review of his life and how the fickle finger of fate had moved and placed him into the bright spotlight of history…

"I was born in Gallup, New Mexico on October 6th, 1925. I was named Hiroshi Miyamura." [n.b. The middle initial "H" was picked up after he began, as a convenience, to use it informally so that "Hershey" would not raise questions among the people he ran into in life.]

Hershey had always thought his hometown was named for the running stride of one of the Southwestern Indian ponies, but I became informed from a site on the Internet that in 1880, a paymaster for the Atlantic and Pacific Railroad, David L. Gallup, established his headquarters along the construction right-of-way of the southern transcontinental route. The railroad workers began "going to Gallup" to get their pay; the town was born and named in 1881.

Hershey

"I am one of seven children. I am the oldest of the two boys and have five sisters. My sisters are: Chiyoko [n.b. She prefers to drop the diminutive 'ko'], born in Kumamoto, Japan in 1920; Momoko, born in Gibson, New Mexico in 1922; the rest of my sisters were born in Gallup: Michiko [Mich], born 1924; Shizuko [Suzi], born in 1928; and Shigeko, born in 1931. My younger brother's name is Kei, who was born in Gallup in 1929. I later learned that I also had one other brother, George, who was born in February, 1927 and survived only a short three days.

"I knew next to nothing about my father's family until just these past few years when I obtained a great deal of information. My father, Yaichi Miyamura, was born in Ogawa-machi, Kumamoto-ken, Japan in 1888, and my mother Tori Matsukawa, was also born in Ogawa-machi, Japan in 1896. My father's sister, Tazu, had emigrated to the U.S. from Kumamoto, Japan with her husband and infant son, Frank, in 1903. She operated four boarding houses in Gamerco, New Mexico four miles north of Gallup, where she housed approximately 300 bachelors, mostly Japanese natives who were miners working in the coal mines."

Investigation on the web for the source for the name Gamerco uncovered the fact that it was quite simply just an acronym for the Gallup American Coal Company.

Hershey

"My father, who was born into a quite wealthy family, was able to travel and came over to the U.S. from Japan in 1906, and arrived in Seattle, Washington. He traveled around the U.S. and Canada for about three years, traveling by rail, exploring the coal-mining industry and working at odd jobs as a casual laborer to expand his knowledge of life in America, and to explore as many facets of living as possible. He eventually arrived in Gamerco, New Mexico in 1909 and resided there with his sister, Tazu. I am not sure what my father did while he was there, but it probably certainly involved helping his sister with the upkeep of her four boarding houses.

"Then my father returned to Kumamoto, Japan in 1912. He was planning to get married, but this was put on hold when he was drafted by the Japanese Army and had to serve for two years.

"Curiously enough, part of my Father's overseas duty was served in Korea. After he was discharged, he married my mother, Tori Matsukawa, on February 16, 1919 and they lived in Ogawa-machi until my eldest sister, Chiyo, was born, on February 28th 1920."

He had discovered the fact that his father and new wife were subjected to some coldness from his father's family because she was considered beneath his family's status and this was a fairly major thing in the Japan of the early 20th century.

"They then decided to emigrate to the United States in 1921 and he returned to the U.S. by ship, arriving in San Francisco in January of 1922.

Hershey

"My father, mother, and sister traveled to Gamerco, New Mexico where my father worked in a coal mine as a coal weigher. He weighed the coal as it came out of the pits. He continued at the mine for a year and then decided that he wanted to own and operate his own business. The family moved four miles south to Gallup, New Mexico and he opened his business in 1923 in a building resembling a railroad boxcar. It was called the Box Car Lunch and was located at 220 West Coal Avenue.

"Since the business was doing so well the landlord [n.b. Dominic Vernetti] negotiated with my father and constructed a larger building at the same address. In 1929 the O.K. Café was opened for business 24 hours a day. The O.K. Café employed a staff of cooks, waitresses, dishwashers and janitorial staff who worked in two shifts, a day-shift and a night-shift. It was popular with the Native Americans, the townspeople and, therefore, a growing number of tourists discovered it."

The Miyamura children relate that since their parents were both in the restaurant business, it was necessary for them to learn English, especially their father, because he had to do all the ordering of supplies in English. Since their parents were not traditionalists, having left Japan because of their differences with the culture there, the children were never required to become fluent in the Japanese language.

The three eldest girls: Chiyo, Momoko, and Michiko, could speak Japanese better than the rest. But Michiko concedes that by the time she, the third child, was learning, she was not very practiced in the subtleties of the language until she married a more traditional Japanese man. Most of the children did understand basic Japanese because they would address their father in English and he would often formulate his reply in his native tongue.

"This is the environment all of us kids grew up in. I remember as a young boy eating in the restaurant, usually without the whole family sitting around the table. Only the evening meal, holidays, and birthdays were we together as a family.

"Up until the sixth grade I was doing fine until a new teacher, Miss Bennet, who could not pronounce my name with ease, so she said she was going to call me 'Hershey.' "

This nickname stuck from then on through high school. Another source relates that he acquired the nickname because all the girls at school thought that he was as sweet as "chocolate."

Hershey

"I had a pretty much normal upbringing as far as school goes but, as I said, I did not have a lot of parental direction and guidance so I did not study much and I did not accomplish too much in school. All I knew how to do was to play and have a good time.

"My younger years were my most memorable years because I was entirely different than I am now. I used to hang around with a bunch of other boys my age. There were between fifteen and twenty of us from time-to-time. The mixture of the group was quite different. They were Italian, Slavic, Mexican, and Anglos. There were only a couple of other Japanese boys my age at school. As little as I was, I used to be a bully, believe it or not. I had some of the other guys bring candy for me. I never was wanting for candy of any kind. I was like this as I went from the sixth through the ninth grades. Then I outgrew that phase of my youth.

"This went on until my mother passed away in 1936 at the age of 39. After she passed away, my father was very busy with the café, as well as tending to the rearing of seven children."

The following was related to the author by Ms. Michiko Yoshida, Hershey's sister. She was recalling conversations she had with Hershey over the years and they are paraphrased here as she remembers the thoughts he expressed:

"My mother was in the hospital and had had surgery when I was eleven years old. Plans were being made for me to attend the Japanese Conference of the Free Methodist Camp and Conference. It was located in Pacific Palisades, California, in the Los Angeles area between Malibu and Santa Monica, just across the Pacific Coast Highway from the Pacific Ocean. At first I was reluctant about leaving, but my mother and Mr. Shinto, the Layman, convinced me she was feeling fine and recovering nicely after her surgery and told me that I should go ahead with my plans to attend the camp. She also told me she would not worry either because I was going with other members from our Gallup Japanese Free Methodist Church.

Hershey

"Just after my arrival and after only one day in California, I had to pack-up and return home immediately, I was told, because my mother had passed away. On my way back to Gallup I had never felt such a sadness and that burden was very difficult for me to bear. But, with time, God heals and He was always in my heart and gave me the strength to overcome the anguish of my memories of this time and her passing."

Michiko continued, saying, "Hersh, my brother, has always been a very humble Christian and has had a deep abiding faith in God his whole life."

Hershey continues. "In 1937 my father decided to relocate to another building three or four doors down the street to a smaller restaurant that was still operated as the O.K. Café, but with hours from 6 a.m. to 11 p.m., seven days a week instead of 24-hours a day. The O.K. Café remained in business until the latter part of 1939.

"Knowing his daughters Momoko and Michiko would be leaving home to attend college after their graduation from Gallup High School, my father had to plan accordingly for the loss in 'manpower.' When he had the opportunity to acquire the smaller Lucky Lunch Café, located on North Third Street, he took it.

"My father purchased the Lucky Lunch Café in 1940 where the business hours were from 7 a.m. until 6 p.m. He operated the Lucky Lunch with Chiyo, my eldest sister.

"Prior to 1940, as I was growing up after my mother passed away, I was under the care of Chiyo, Momoko, and Michiko. My sisters Suzi, Shigeko, and brother Kei were also supervised by them. This is because my father's business still required most of his time. Chiyo helped with the cooking and my other sisters took turns working as waitresses at the restaurant. Kei and I also used to have chores that we had to do in the family business, usually on Saturdays.

"I went out for various sports in school, but the coaches never gave me a chance to show my talent because they thought I was too small and too light to be a good football player which is what I really wanted to play.

Hershey

"I went out for track for a while and then discovered boxing. Boxing just seemed to come naturally for me and I enjoyed it very much. I used to go around with my gloves hanging over my shoulder looking for people to give me a challenge. I had a few high school boxing matches and almost made the Amateur Golden Gloves team. But by then the Second World War had broken out and because I was Japanese, I was not really in the running. I weighed between 110-112 pounds for most of that time. That went on for a year or so. The 20-30 club used to sponsor boxing tournaments in those days and I blamed my boxing career and one incident in school for causing my life to change.

"I think I was in the sixth grade when I got hit in the head with a baseball bat by a big black girl swinging it around. She didn't see me and hit me in the back of the head and I thought she knocked my head off. I don't know how long I was out but they told me it was an hour or so.

"The other incident was during one of the amateur boxing matches. The ropes around the ring were very loose, and I stepped back and fell through them and landed on my head. Those two incidents caused me to change, personality-wise. I never again was the aggressive kid who I had been."

Hershey

His younger brother Kei provided another slant on the incident as follows: "I remember one time Hersh was boxing for the 20-30 club and he was fighting an Indian named Begay. I remember him and they got into a clinch and when the Indian pushed him away, the ropes were so loose they just spread open and Hersh flew out of the ring onto his back. I was with Richard Shinto and he said

'Go see what happened.' I said I didn't want to because people were all crowded around him. He hurt himself that time."

"My father's sister's son, my cousin, Frank Uyeda, was a master mechanic and my mother had wanted me to learn how to repair cars, so when I turned fifteen and continuing on in my sixteenth year, I worked for him during the summer months at his shop for no pay or anything, trying to learn the ropes on how to be an automobile mechanic. When I turned seventeen, my last year in school, I was working as a mechanic at the Ford agency in Gallup.

"It was about this time that I met Amelio DiGregorio. He was a year older than I. I really hadn't gotten to know him that well until this time, right before he left to join the Army. I remember going to his house a lot and his dad used to make wine and always offered me some. He made good wine. Back in those days the Italian people were all famous for making their own wine. I ate at his house a lot of times!

"I liked Amelio because he was kind of loud, always said what was on his mind, and he always thought that he was right. His loud talk never bothered me that much and we got along real well and we really understood each other.

Hershey

"We really didn't get into trouble together. My getting-into-trouble-phase was when I was somewhat younger, it was more like we were into a lot of mischief!

"He was a good-hearted guy and always tried to help people that were down. Whenever we saw someone that was down and out he would give them a buck or two.

"He went into the service before I did and he would write and tell me what was going on over there in Europe. His brother was there at the same time. So we kept in contact through correspondence until he came home.

"Then while I was off in Korea, he and his wife Anna Jean took care to look after Terry. Amelio taught Terry how to drive and helped her if she needed anything done around the house. He was also my best man at my wedding.

"After I came home from Korea, he went to Washington along with his wife, Anna Jean, for the Medal of Honor ceremonies. My other friend, Dan L. McKinney and his wife, Joyce Ann, also accompanied me to the Capitol.

"When a new development opened up east of town, Amelio and I were the first two to buy homes in the development, right next to each other. Then when his brother bought a home, he bought the home on the other side of me, so I was sandwiched in-between both of the brothers.

"Our families shared a lot of backyard barbeques and picnics and my daughter used to play next door with Amelio's daughter who was older than her.

Hershey

"Amelio also was kind enough, when Terry could not travel with me, like when she was having one of our children, and I had a previously scheduled event that I was attending, to accompany me to several veteran functions and conventions.

"Amelio got to know all of my friends, especially all my Japanese-American friends from the veteran functions we attended together.

"I really hated to lose him when he passed away on August 21, 1995. He always had heart problems, but he died of an aneurism in his stomach and passed away within minutes.

"Let me see, where was I, oh, I just went on through Gallup High School, which had about 300 kids, and I graduated with my class of about 50 other seniors on May 21, 1943."

In one of those quirky footnotes to history: although Hershey completed all of his schooling in Gallup, none of the buildings exist today. The elementary and junior high schools were razed to make room for a new federal building and his high school burned down. It is a good bet that there are institutions of higher learning that are thankful that he did not matriculate to their campuses.

Hershey

10

At this point in his chronicle, members of Hershey's family demanded equal time to put some of Hershey's recollection of events of his childhood into perspective:

Michiko related to the author, "Suzi, Shig, and Kei were always getting into trouble because the big kids were off playing and left them to entertain themselves."

Shizuko said, "When we got into trouble, my father would always say, 'You're the oldest, it's your fault,' and Kei would just smirk at me and laugh with his eyes behind my father's back."

Chiyo Herrera, the eldest daughter, was born in Kumamoto, Japan in 1920, and immigrated to the United States with her parents. She went to school in the Gallup schools and married her husband, John, on June 7th, 1937. They had four children: Nancy, born in 1940, who became a bookkeeper and has worked for various employers; Michael, born in 1944, found his life's employment at the El Paso Natural Gas Plant in Gallup; John, born in 1946, who after serving in Vietnam, went on to a career at Safeway, and finally, after further studies as an Electrical Engineer, is now employed at the Marriot Hotel in San Francisco's Embarcadero Center; and finally Gerald, born in 1956, who enrolled in an electronics study course at DeVry Institute, and after many years at Litton Industries, now owns his own retail computer sales and support business.

Hershey

Chiyo is noted as the family librarian, not historian, as that honor falls upon Michiko. Chiyo has numerous bookcases in her home and hundreds of books on all subjects. She is partial to history, but most of the collection is comprised of popular best sellers. She also has a extensive collection of music, updated as technology has advanced. Her favorite album is the opera, Madame Butterfly by Puccini, with emphasis on the aria *Un bel di* [n.b. One Fine Day].

She also notes that Hershey, being the first born son of the family, was 'spoiled' rotten, as is the tradition in Japanese families. He was his mother's favorite and when he was younger, could get almost anything he wanted by plying his elders with tearful entreaties. She says this without rancor and admits that she has always loved and respected Hershey, especially for his heroic achievements in Korea and his powerful and informative talks at his subsequent participation in patriotic and veteran functions.

Hershey

Momoko Saruwatari, the second eldest daughter, was born in Gibson, New Mexico in 1922, and after the family moved to Gallup, studied her way through high school there, and then married her husband, Ben, on June 6th 1943 at Delta, Colorado. She was enrolled at the Barnes School of Business in Denver and she became an accomplished bookkeeper. Originally, she had desired to go to Texas and take up studies that would enable her to become a school teacher, but the advent of the Second World War with its concomitant distrust and mistreatment of Japanese-Americans precluded that.

Momoko is an enthusiastic runner and has participated in nine of the renowned twelve kilometer "Bay-to-Breakers" run/walk-a-thons in the San Francisco area, seven of those in the "over 65" category. Her desire is to participate in one more, to bring her total to ten of the events, but her chance of running in the last one in July 2001, was hampered by the anniversary excursion to 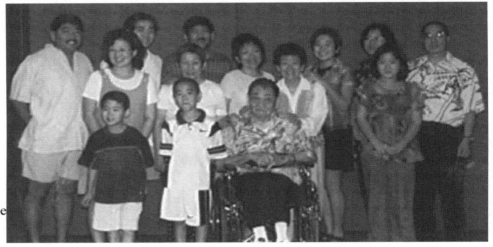 Korea, where she accompanied other family members and her brother Hershey to the observances. Now nearing eighty, she is not sure that she is up to the stress of ever completing that tenth challenge.

Their children: Judi, born in 1944, is a writer of various genre and an architectural designer; the first born son, Jack, was born in 1946, and after a stint in the Air Force at Misawa Air Base, Japan, went into sales, and eventually bought his own printing business; Linda Joy, the second daughter, was born in 1951 and, after schooling, became a financial analyst and is now pursuing her career at UCSF in San Francisco; the last son, Corky, was born in 1956 and has had a long career in sales in the beverage industry.

Hershey

Momoko worked in the family restaurants between the ages of thirteen and eighteen. She would go to work early in the morning before school and clean the tables and do other chores, such as filling the condiment containers. She would also help with the coal stove that was used for cooking and had to be lit and stoked to get it to the proper temperature for preparing the meals.

At one time, she had wanted to quit school and dedicate her time to the business after her mother passed away, but her father would not allow her to make that unwise decision, talking her into "staying the course."

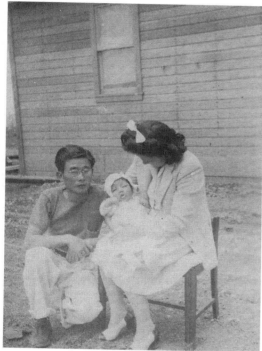

Being occupied at the family business so much of the time, she did not spend that much time with Hershey. She does remember that as the first born son, he was somewhat "spoiled" and would sometimes ensconce himself behind the coal stove in the kitchen when he did not get his way and was behaving like this in the process of healing his wounded spirits.

Michiko Yoshida, nicknamed Mich, or Miki when she was a child, is married to Paul. She is the third eldest of the seven children. She was born and raised in Gallup, New Mexico in 1924 and went through high school there.

She was twelve when her mother passed away and she had to assume some of the responsibility for raising the family and doing things that normally would not be expected of a young girl. But she had been raised with responsibility for chores and, remembering how and what her mother did, helped her older sisters in continuing to raise the family.

Hershey

She thought it was a lot of fun growing up, but during an interview, laughingly said she did not know how her younger siblings viewed all this enjoyment she was having raising them. She felt the experience was quite rewarding and thought it was fun watching the youngsters growing up, even in the absence of her mother.

She always thought her father did an excellent job as head of the household and she admired him a lot as a child. She says that because of all the household responsibilities and expected assistance in the restaurant, she was kept busy and did not have the opportunity to dwell on the loss of her mother, and thus her sorrow was eased.

She thinks that because her mother and father were so close and worked so hard that they provided the example that all of the children eventually emulated. She found out later how, because her father had married below his station in Japan, he moved, leaving his family, to bring his wife and daughter to America where there were no social stigmas associated with the love that he had for her.

Her father did, even with all of his hours out of the home, maintain his position as the head of the family and took an active interest and hand in the shaping of his children's lives. All the children, when referring to their father, state that his word was law, so they did not lack for a guiding hand, which was how things were done in Japan where their father was born and raised.

Michiko also thought her father was a very broad-minded and wise man. He always maintained an attitude, even through the Depression, that whatever life dealt you, you had to face the challenge and overcome any hardship so that you could prevail. Thus Michiko accepted the challenge of caring for the younger children without trepidation. Seeing this from the eyes of the younger children, they have said that Mich also ruled with an iron hand. So she *had* grasped the lessons that her father had been teaching through his guidance and discipline.

Hershey

She did not think that having to accept this extra responsibility cheated her out any meaningful enjoyment as a young girl. This, she says, is because "Number one, the children had to be taken care of and I knew my father did not want to see any of us separated when my mother passed away. This was very important to him."

After graduation from high-school she entered Barnes School of Business in Denver, mostly because her oldest sister Momoko was already enrolled there. This was during the Second World War. The girls were to be together to satisfy their father's desires.

Hershey drove her to Denver where she remained only a couple of months. Then she wrote to her father and informed him that business school was not her choice for a career. "I told him that I wanted to go into nursing. So, I was going to return to Gallup."

Michiko's husband, Paul Yoshida, who at age twenty in Gardena, California, had had about 48-hours to decide whether to become a prisoner at an internment camp in California, or leave for Denver, where Governor Ralph L. Carr [n.b. Republican, Governor from 1939-1943] had announced the unpopular policy that Colorado would welcome all Americans to their state. He decided to relocate to Denver.

Hershey

His parents unfortunately lost their home, constructed on two acres, and their produce market, the Ranch Market, at Western and Imperial Highway in the Los Angeles area. He did not know what pittance the home was "stolen" for, nor the name of the fine, "upstanding American" who graciously took it off their hands for peanuts. But he did know that the market had to be sold, with all of its inventory and equipment, at the last minute for $500 to a Chinese businessman.

Paul met his future wife, Michiko, in 1942 when he was 21 years old at a YWCA in Denver. She was with her older sister Momoko and he was accompanied by a friend of his. The boys, after talking the pros and cons over between themselves, boldly struck up a conversation with the two lovely girls and ended up walking them home.

Paul and Michiko dated a couple of times and then she told him she was going back to Gallup. Paul told her he had been through Gallup, "That's somewhere in Wyoming, isn't it?" When he learned it was in New Mexico, he still thought he had been through it because he had also visited New Mexico and the name is unique enough that it stuck in his mind.

When Michiko announced she was going to return to New Mexico, Paul got up the courage to ask her to marry him. In his words, "You can't do that. I just got to know you. And somehow or another I talked her into, hey, let's get married then, and she said, 'O.K. let's go then.' " This prompted much laughter and protestation from Michiko during his relating of this version of their courtship and his proposal.

They have two children; a daughter Patricia [Patsy] born in 1944 and a son, Alan, born in 1951. Patsy has retired from the University of Irvine and her husband, Sam Shimamura, retired as a Professor of Pharmacy at UC San Francisco to join the staff at the Western University of Health Science at Pomona, California. He currently is the Assistant Dean there. He is also on the Board of Directors of the American Society of Health-System Pharmacists and attends meetings once a month in Bethesda, Maryland.

Hershey

Paul and Michiko's son, Alan, is a Mastering Engineer for the music industry. According to his mother, he takes tremendous pride in his work and is very good at what he does. Recently, he has taken up bicycling as a hobby. Unfortunately for him, he happens to live in the Los Feliz area of Los Angeles, which coincidentally, Stacy, the daughter of Michiko's younger brother, Kei, maintains as her assigned police patrol responsibility, so the family can keep an eye on him. [Uttered amid much merriment among the family members during their interview.]

Shizuko "Suzi" Tashiro [the younger sister between Hershey and Kei], was born in 1928 and raised in Gallup, New Mexico. She left Gallup when she was twenty and went to California to go to school but got married instead. She has four children: Ron, born in 1951, is a Deputy Sheriff in Southern California; Kerry, born in 1953, works in Civil Service for the County in Phoenix, Arizona; Shelly, born in 1956, supervises the delicatessen at a major supermarket in

Southern California; and Blythe, born in 1957, owns her own business in Phoenix, Arizona. Shizuko has eight grandchildren, one great-grandson and one great-granddaughter. None of her children have married Japanese-Americans.

She doesn't remember her mother very much because she passed away when Suzi was only eight years old. One memory that sticks in her mind was one time her mother made her some soup and made her eat it before she was allowed to go to see a movie with her older sister. Suzi was five or six at the time.

She also remembers that she had a favorite dress and was going to a friend's for dinner, but the dress was dirty. Her mother washed and pressed her dress for her before she left.

Hershey

One Christmas, Shizuko, and her younger sister Shigeko got dolls, big ones, and a baby-buggy. But Shizuko didn't like her doll and wanted her younger sister's doll instead of the one she got and her mother switched them for her. That is about the extent of her memories of her mother.

Shizuko remembers that to her, she was big, but not tall. She also remembers that her mother laughed and smiled a lot. She remarked that if she didn't see pictures of her, she doesn't think she would really, truly remember what she looked like. But her mother's laughter sticks out in her memory.

She doesn't remember whether her mother or father had more influence over her as a child because she was pretty much raised under the supervision of the older children. She laughingly remembers Hersh's style as, "You're my little sister and you are going to do this right...and you're going to do it now!"

According to Shizuko, two events jump to memory from when Hershey returned home after his initial training in the Army during World War II. The first is that when he came home on leave, he was sporting a new pipe. She thought that he probably assumed that this made him look more like a man of the world. The second recollection was that he offered to pay her $0.25 to iron a pair of his pants, and this seemed to her to mean that he had a lot of money to throw around at the time.

Hershey

As Shizuko got older, her father ruled with an iron hand and that was for sure. She knew that if she did something wrong, her dad was going to be there and do something about it. "So there was a certain amount of trepidation that you didn't want to get Dad mad. He was the type of man that he could look at you and you knew you were going to get it."

Her father was a very strict man but he was also very open and broad-minded. She does remember fondly that he was an excellent cook. She retains a vivid memory of this, especially his doughnuts. She thought he made the best doughnuts and biscuits that you ever wanted to eat. She used to sneak up after he had baked a batch. She thought she was so smart. One of the waitresses took the fresh doughnuts and put them into the counter case and Shizuko snuck up feeling quite secure that, since she was shorter than the counter, she could not be seen. But she said what she didn't realize was that when the little fingers reached up to snatch a doughnut the patrons and staff could see her hand. There was this very intimidating waitress who caught her one day and said, "What do you think you are doing?" It pretty much put a crimp into the doughnut pilfering crime-wave.

Shizuko admired her dad and does not think she has ever met a man who was his equal. She speculates that is why the children all grew up with such a sense of independence and respect for the truth.

Shigeko, "Shige," Sasaki [the youngest sister] was born in 1931 and brought up in Gallup, New Mexico, where she attended school, and got married at the age of 21 to Narumi Sasaki. They were divorced in 1979.

Hershey

105

Their children are: Randall Craig, born in 1952, is in management at the Post Office in Oxnard, California; Ryan Kent, born in 1957, who retired from the U.S. Air Force, is presently a computer technician and consultant; Candice, "Dee Dee," born in 1959, is a school teacher; Jody, "Joey," born in 1961, a karate black-belt master and six-time champion, now owns and operates his own dojo; Todd Miles, born in 1963, an officer in the U.S. Air Force and graduate of the Air Force Academy in Colorado Springs, Colorado, currently is attending Command School in Montgomery, Alabama; and, Crystal, born in 1964, is now a computer programmer and analyst.

One of the most powerful memories Shigeko has of Hershey is that when he was returning to San Francisco from Korea, as the ship was preparing to dock, the band struck up a patriotic air, which one she does not remember, but she does recall that there was not a dry eye in the entire group waiting on the quay for the arrival of the Marine Adder. Then after docking, here came her brother, walking down the gangplank all by himself and he had a noticeable limp. This was when she first realized that he had been wounded in Korea.

Kei Miyamura, the second son, was born in Gallup, New Mexico in 1929 and went to school through high school there. When he was six or seven, Hersh handed him a football and then told him run straight for him and when he did, Hersh evaded his dash causing him to fall. It

knocked the breath out of him. Because of his big brother spending the time teaching him how to run, evade tackles, and handle the football, Kei went on to became an accomplished football player. Hershey also took the time to put the gloves on him and instructed him in the rudiments of how to box.

Hershey

Kei became a three-year letterman in football and boxing. He was only 5'5" tall and weighed in at a mere 117 pounds and yet, was the first-string Varsity quarterback in his junior and senior years. "We only lost two games out of those 20 games and they were both to Albuquerque High. We couldn't beat Albuquerque High."

Shizuko related, "He was so small, they would say, 'Here comes that little wiry Kei!' " His father would yell from the stands, "Go, go, GO!" His father, even with the work entailed in running the restaurant, never missed one of Kei's games. "Every game that I played, he was there."

Referring to when he was much younger, one day, Kei, while not old enough to drive, was playing in his father's 1939 Mercury. He had taken the keys and started it up. Then he would drive it straight forward a short distance, then put it into reverse and back it straight up to the starting point [n.b. This must obviously have been one of the new-fangled automatic transmissions]. Shizuko, a year younger than

him, tempted and dared him into driving the car to town with her as a passenger. Once downtown, Kei decided to try and turn around to go back and Shizuko helped him turn the wheel. They collided with the pipes that guard the gas pumps at a service station in town and scraped the side of the car up. "You know I didn't think about the brakes and stuff like that, cause I was just a kid. Boy, we took the car back and parked it and we never touched it again!"

He did not reveal to the authors, the level nor fashion of his punishment for that act of dauntlessness.

Hershey

One of the most memorable remembrances that Kei retains of Hershey is that when Kei was fifteen years old, he and Hershey were playing out in the yard and Hershey called him over and said, "You go to Dad and tell him to give you $300 because I am going take you to buy a car."

Kei said, "I went in and I told my dad what he said and I got the money and we went to town and he bought me my first car when I was fifteen years old. I remember that it was really something driving to junior high with all of the guys who were my buddies."

When asked if he looked up to Hershey as a role model, Kei replied, "Well not really, because he would really treat me rough. That is why I got to be pretty tough myself. Whenever I had to fight in school, it got so no one ever bothered me again. But, when I was young he used to treat me rough. He wanted me to grow up to be a man, not a baby. Other than that he treated me good."

Then Kei went out to California where he met his future wife, Kimi, at a Boy Scout dance. He was not a Boy Scout, as he was nineteen-years old at the time, and was just hanging around outside with some of his crowd. There were not enough boys to go around at the dance, so the hangers-on were asked if they wanted to come in and dance. Kei, once two or three others agreed to go in with him, saw Kimi, who was sixteen years old at the time. He was struck with wonderment at her pulchritude, and that, as the saying goes, is the end of that tune!

"I married Kimi in 1951 and we had two children. My firstborn was Stacy, born in 1959. She is a Los Angeles Police officer and head of her unit. She was an Explorer Scout and she was kind of naughty and ditched school a lot, a typical teenager. These two policemen who were school cops took an interest in her and guided her, and that is how she ended up being a cop."

One of the family joined in and said, "She knew most of the officers, so it was natural that she joined the cops." This utterance was accompanied with much laughter amongst them. Their youngest daughter, Shari, was born in 1966 and they lost her to an illness in 1977.

The family remembrances continue: When still at the O.K. Café, Kei and Shizuko, would Hershey go up the stairway where the buildings were all built adjoining one another. They would run from one end of the block to the other over the roofs with the sound of their footsteps resounding through all the businesses. Finally their father came up to the roof and told them, "You can't do that; I don't want you up there, etc. etc." Then pretty soon the kids, being kids, would again be running across the roofs and did it one time too many. They got caught by their father who took them down into the cellar under the restaurant where all the canned goods and supplies were stored. It was dark, really pitch-black. My father said, "You are going to stay down here until I tell you can come up."

Right at the bottom of the door, a small sliver of light peeped through and Kei and Shizuko, who were scared, sat on the steps looking at the meager light, waiting until someone came to let them out. Finally their father let them out and Kei who was scared to death came running out and their father laughed at their fright. Needless to say they never went up to the roof to play "run down the whole block" again, at least the memory does not linger, if they did so.

Shizuko says, "Hersh never got the bawlings out and all. He was smart enough to stay out of trouble and he was working at his cousin's part-time learning to be a mechanic."

But Hershey does not come out of his childhood totally unscathed. The children relate that there was a Japanese family who made tofu and would take it around to the other Japanese families and sell it to them. Their father would buy it and make what the kids called "Japanese Stew." This meant that it had everything in it but the kitchen sink.

Dear reader, you can probably relate to this because even in our family we had a similar experience, except in our case it was labeled, "Leftover Soup." It was always avoided if at all possible with as inventive of an excuse as we were capable of producing as we were growing up. This inventiveness and frugality, I think, was a by-product of the hard times engendered by the Great Depression.

Anyway, continuing, when their father prepared this meal for the family, the kids, following the example of Hershey and Shigeko who sat next to the wall which had a fairly sizeable hole in it, would slip the undesired portion of the comestible off of their plates and down through that hole.

That was not all. Sometimes the meals that were prepared for them were so terrible in the eyes of the children that one of them would go and keep and eye on their father. Hershey would collect all the food that they wanted to make "gone" and when the lookout signaled that the coast was clear from their father's observation, he would hustle it into the back and deposit it into a "slop-bucket" that resided there.

Their father would set the kids down and say, "Now you eat!" When he checked back on Hershey them he was always prideful of their appetites and the gusto with which they dispatched what they often saw as his economically-minded, gastronomically lackluster creations.

The kids stated that the wall never had a bad smell coming from it and they attribute this to either rats who lived under the building, or to the fact that the space behind the wall was quite deep. Their father went to his grave never knowing the desecration that had befallen his culinary inventiveness.

Shizuko says, "Hersh wasn't an angel; he was just smart and never got caught. I think that at times he had some of the qualities of leadership. We would play in a group and play 'Follow the Leader.' Hersh was always the leader. I blame him and Kei for the fact that I was raised as a tomboy. I was always playing with the group of boys in the neighborhood because there were not many girls my age.

"This one time he took us all around and finally up on the roof of the garage where he jumped off. It was my turn and I looked down and I thought, 'I'm not going to do that.'

"The guys were Kei, Billy Shinto, Tom Kimura, Jack Shinto, and Ben Shima... Anyway I was always the only girl so if I wanted to play, I had to act like a boy. So there I was standing there and Hersh said, 'Jump!' and I said, 'No I'm not going to jump!' He said, 'If you don't jump, I'm going to come up there and push you off. You want to jump off or be pushed off?' I jumped! That is the way he was.

"Another time, Hersh had put boxing gloves on me and I was boxing one of the neighborhood boys, Ted Shima. All the guys were surrounding us and cheering us on. Hersh was saying, 'Give him a right! Give him a left...' he was refereeing. Anyway my dad came out and he saw me boxing. I was never so embarrassed in my life. He came out and pulled the gloves off of me and he pulled them off with such force that I sat right down on my tail-end. He looked at Hersh and said, 'Don't you ever put gloves on her again!', and then he turned to me and said, 'You are a girl not a boy and you don't do this!' I never boxed again. That's the kind of brother that I had."

Kei recollects, "One time Hersh came flying up from the seven steps out of the cellar and I called, 'Where're you going?' Well, right behind him came my father carrying a stout stick and chasing him. Hersh exited out the backdoor and went streaking down the alley out of sight."

At this point in his narration, Shizuko interjected, "Do you know why he was chasing Hersh?"

"No," replied Kei.

Shizuko continued, "We were playing 'Crack the Whip, and Hersh whipped me very Hershey hard and when he did he twisted my arm. I started crying and Hersh said, 'Why are you crying?' 'Because my arm hurts; I can't lift my arm.' Well, when I started crying, Pop came out and he said, 'What is going on?' I told him that Hersh hurt my arm and I said I can't move it and that is when Hersh took off. My father chased him clear down the alley to the corner and he outran my dad."

"Boy I tell you they came flying out of the cellar and I was wondering what went on," says Kei.

"Well," Shizuko said, "that is what it was all about."

If you look at a map of the Navajo Nation, you will see that Gallup is surrounded by the Navaho Indian Reservation.

When cooking for the visiting Indians during the Indian Ceremonial, a Pow-Wow of the tribes from all over the nation, the Lucky Lunch Café prepared a much touted stew and served it with mash potatoes and gravy, four slices of bread, some vegetables, two cups of coffee and a dessert. It was served on a very large plate and cost only a quarter.

One time an Indian finished eating, and decided he was going sneak out the back without paying. Shizuko hollered out to Hersh, "That guy is leaving and didn't pay!"

"That Indian was a big guy, but Hersh ran after him and tackled him and collected the quarter for the dinner. Although he was smaller, he was not going to allow his father to be cheated out of his money."

The restaurant had such a reputation with the Indians for good cooking that they would come and line-up outside, waiting patiently to be seated, sometimes for hours at a time. During this particular celebration, Hershey, now about sixteen years old, would man the door and when one of the sisters would tell him that two customers had departed out the backdoor, "O.K. Hersh, two out!" Hershey would unlock the door and allow two more customers into the dining room through the front.

Hershey

During these days of the Pow-Wow celebration, the kids would have to lock the door while the family stopped at midday to eat. The Indians would wait outside patiently until they were done and then the parade would recommence.

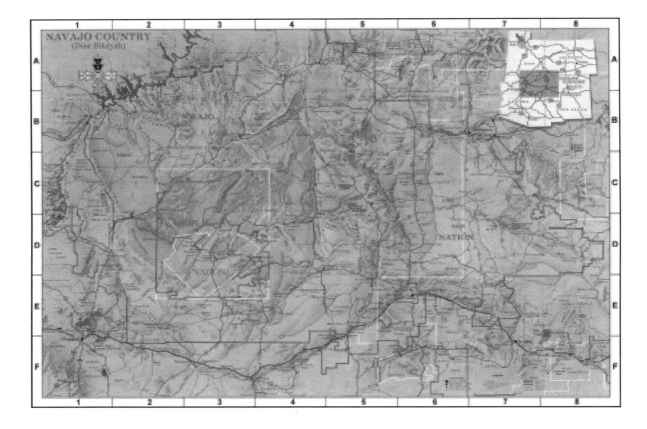

They served so many meals that sometimes their father would take in $200 in a day. That works out to 800 meals served, and if you have ever been in the business, that is a lot of meals for a small restaurant that sat less than 30 customers at a time.

The kids would cleanup the dining area after they ate. Kei used to sweep up the floor after the family meal. One time he found a $20 bill on the floor. This insured that he would always be available to clean up the floor.

In his words, "I'LL SWEEP!!" Now that was an industrious youngster, yes?

Hershey

11

Hershey, tired and groggy from all of his meandering down memory lane, cleaned up and joined Terry in the bedroom for some well-earned sleep. Upon rising the next morning, and while driving toward Tsalie Lake, his mind, not occupied by the scenery since it was still dark, again began weaving down the halls of his memory…

"After another seven years this friend of mine [n.b. Ed Junker], I didn't know him that well then, but he was a Bataan veteran of World War II. [n.b. a reference to U.S. and Filipino troops captured on the Philippine island of Bataan in April 1942 by the Japanese in World War II, who underwent a brutal "death march" to a prison camp; thousands died on the march.] He was a prisoner of the Japanese in World War II. But he knew who I was and we got acquainted and he came to me one day and said that his company was opening up a new service station west of Gallup, and that it was going to be near the interchange, [n.b. junction of the famous Route 66 and the road north to Gamerco] and would I be interested in opening it up. I told him yes because I really was looking for something else to do. I couldn't see myself staying in the auto-parts business which I really didn't care that much for. The owner of White Auto Store offered to sell me half-interest in it if I stayed, but I told him I had to try the new station.

"All of my friends, including even my wife Terry, tried to talk me out of it saying that this company was unknown, Humble Oil Company, 'Happy Motoring.' What the heck was that?

"Well they said, 'Naw you will never make it.' This station was three miles west of Gallup and in just about three blocks more there was nothing much west of Gallup for many miles in those days. But I said, 'I still have to try it.'

"I opened that station in December of 1960 during a snow storm. Even then I had a large number of customers and I sold a whole lot of gas … that, I couldn't believe.

"I enjoyed that kind of work because I was able to work on automobiles as well as meet the public. It was a new environment for me so I … twenty-five years went by so fast.

"My kids grew up and all graduated and left Gallup before I even realized what was happening. I was so involved in that business, because I was kept so busy from morning to night. I hardly got to see any of my children. That went on until after they were gone. The last one, my daughter Kelly, left in 1974.

"I soon got the word that the company was going to raise my rent again and in those

Hershey

days, this was in 1984, the cars were changing – they were coming more into electronics and my equipment was outdated for these new cars.

"I thought since the company was going to raise my rent, and I was going to have to buy new equipment, I couldn't see where I would be gaining too much there, so I said it was time for me to retire.

"Before I did, I asked the company if I could buy the station, or I told them, I was going to get out of the business. They said they didn't want to sell the station, so once I signed, I had five days to get out, and so that is what happened.

"I got out of the business in April 1984. It was kind of a forced retirement, but it was something I was sort of looking forward to anyway. After almost 25 years in the service-station business I thought I deserved the rest, although someone didn't feel I needed it [during his interview, he turned and was looking directly at his wife, Terry] and thought I should continue working. To this day she hasn't convinced me of that...

"From that time on I was able to attend more veteran functions... conventions and stuff like that, which I have been doing since then. I haven't been getting involved in the working and operations of any organizations but at least showing my face and attending.

"I've been asked to get politically involved in Gallup, but I said I'm not a politician, that is the furthest thing in
my mind.

"That's about all I have been doing...going to a lot of conventions... reunions... and doing a lot of fishing. I stick to lake fishing and mainly trout.

"I found out I am not a deep-sea fisherman. I went out deep-sea fishing for ten days in Mexico and for the entire ten days I was sick. Every day I went out I got sick. I have been asked to go out again, on several occasions... in Hawaii and on the West Coast. But, here is the part that I don't quite understand... when we boarded the ship to go to Korea from Japan, it was the roughest water a lot of the other servicemen said they had ever seen. The Korean soldiers who had been training with us in Japan were all laying all over the ship, sick. It didn't bother me a bit.

"Going to Italy on the ship and coming back, I never got sick one bit, not even one day. Yet just coming back from Korea, on the smoothest water you could ever find, I was knocked flat for eleven of the nineteen days.

"But...have you ever been on a Liberty ship? Down on the bottom... just the smell. Five tiers of bunks and I am on the bottom. Then you get in line for chow and just the smell of that

Hershey

food… I spent a lot of miserable days on that ship. From that time on it seemed to have done something to my stomach, or my mind, because I haven't been able to get on a ship or a boat after that. I can get on a lake and it doesn't bother me, but the water is not… but on that fishing trip I didn't think I was going to get sick but… I kept saying, 'Tomorrow it will change; it will get better.' But it went on for ten days and never did get better.

"Now I am able to visit my children and their grandchildren and spend more time with them. Our oldest son Mike is married to Marianne Beleele, formerly from Texas. They have two beautiful daughters, Megan and Marisa. Mike is a graphic artist and his wife is a school teacher. They live in Ontario, California. Our second son Pat is a dentist in Kailua, Hawaii since 1984 and is married to Jill Bert, formerly from Kansas. She works as a senior analyst for Hawaii Health Information Corp. They have a son, Ian and a daughter named Madison. Our daughter Kelly is a speech therapist. She is married to Clay Hildahl and they live in the suburbs of Minneapolis. I'm trying to make up for the time I did not spend with them while they were growing up.

"Over time, my brother, Kei, left New Mexico for California as did four of my sisters. My oldest sister and I are the only ones left in Gallup. My mother and father are both buried here in Gallup.

"Right now what I think is left of the Japanese-American population here are my relations, my cousin's offspring and his sister's offspring. Most of the Japanese who settled here in Gallup were, and some remain, in business here."

"I have been truly blessed because my father and mother chose to live in America. My parents had seven children and we are all living and our children are all successful in all of their endeavors. I have also been blessed with a wonderful wife and three great children and grand children. My faith in God saw me through both World War II and the Korean War, and I feel he continues to watch over me today."

Hershey

Hershey

12

During those intervening years, after returning home and settling down, Hershey participated in parades, where he was often the Grand Marshal, events that included the opening of a Korean War Veterans Memorial in Los Angeles, and a Medal of Honor Museum in Riverside, California. He has spoken at countless gatherings of veterans and those interested in hearing his story, told by him, the recipient of the Congressional Medal of Honor.

As this book was nearing completion, he and 183 other Japanese-American Korean War Veterans were revisiting and touring South Korea in May of 2001, and he was taken on a tour of Pan Mun Jom's Freedom Village. Some limited highlights of these fleeting years follow:

"Hiroshi Hershey Miyamura, recipient of the Congressional Medal of Honor, the highest military award an American citizen can win for a deed of personal bravery and self-sacrifice, above and beyond the call of duty — was a visitor in Los Angeles recently for the biennial convention of the Congressional Medal of Honor Society at the Ambassador Hotel.

"Miyamura was one of 200 Medalists attending the three-day convention of this exclusive group, so exclusive that only one in 10,000 ever gets it. Along with a Negro, a Hungarian-born Jew, an American Indian, was Miyamura, a Nisei from Gallup, N.M.

Hershey

"Many of his former 100th Battalion buddies especially from Dog Company, gave Mr. and Mrs. Miyamura a dinner at Imperial Gardens where they listened to Miyamura's experiences in the Korean conflict and as a POW of the North Koreans for 27 months.

"Miyamura lives with his wife and three children in Gallup, where he operates a service station."

He returned to Korea, in 1975 for the first reunion of Korean War Veterans, the 25th anniversary of the onset of hostilities, between September 25th and October 2nd.

The combat action that earned him the award of the Congressional Medal of Honor was memorialized with a 36"
by 48" painting titled, "Portrait of Hiroshi Miyamura," all in blue tones, rendered with acrylic paints, painted by artist George Akimoto, completed in March of 1977 and which is now hanging in the Army Art Collection, U.S. Army Center
of Military History, Ft. Benning, Georgia. This painting is the one depicted on the cover of the book.

There is an overpass on Route 66, "Miyamura Overpass," and a city/state park complex near the overpass that was dedicated in Gallup, New Mexico, March 21st, 1979.

Hershey served as the Grand Marshall of the parade during the 42nd Annual Nisei Week, Japanese Festival in Little Tokyo, Los Angeles, in August 1982.

Hershey was honored at the Japanese-American National Museum Inaugural Dinner at the Westin Bonaventure Hotel in Los Angeles on October the 18th, 1985.

"Honor, Duty, Country," a play about Hershey's exploits, was written by Jon Shiroda and awarded the City of Los Angeles, Culture Affairs Department's grant for 1998. The play's premier performances were on the 6th and 7th of June, 1998 at the Japan American Theater.

Hershey

On April 12th, 1999, the Harold Runnel's Swimming Complex, the 2K Art Gallery, We The People Gallery, and Memory Lane Gallery were opened in Miyamura Park, in Gallup, New Mexico and this collection of facilities was designated the Miyamura Park Complex.

On June 11th, 1999, at a 442nd/100th Battalion Veterans Group reunion in Branson, Missouri, Hershey accepted the key to Branson on behalf of all Nikkei Veterans, [n.b. the term Nikkei is used to describe the four generations of people of Japanese ancestry in America] from the Mayor, Louis Schaeffer. It was reported that Hershey regaled the crowd with a fantastic imitation of Elvis Presley, which was the first time he had ever performed publicly at one of his conventions. His performance rated rave reviews from the attendees who were flabbergasted by this heretofore hidden side of the usually shy Hershey.

One of the other reunion members, upon returning to the West Coast, told Michiko, "I didn't know you had a celebrity in the family." Everyone was talking about it and upon hearing this, the family was stunned. Saying things like, "We were in shock!" "I could not imagine he would go up on stage and do something like that." "My brother, you are talking about my brother?"

As a sad sidelight to his trip to Branson, while there, or at the departure or arrival airport, someone stole his Medal of Honor and it was never recovered. Hershey has since had it replaced, but the original was obviously imbued with many memories.

To make matters worse, Hershey was leaving Branson, bound for Indianapolis, Indiana for a dedication of a wall composed of 27 curved segments, with the names the Medal of Honor recipients etched on them. Hershey contacted a Medal winner in Indianapolis, who in turn contacted a recipient's son in Dallas, who air expressed his deceased father's medal for Hershey to wear during the ceremonies.

The Medal of Honor Society Convention in Riverside, California from October 30th through November 7th, 1999 honored Hershey among the other recipients of the Congressional Medal of Honor.

Hershey

Hershey presided at the Korean Memorial dedication at the Japanese Culture Center Plaza in Los Angeles California, on May 24th, 1997.

The 50th Anniversary convention of the Japanese-American Korean War Veterans was dedicated as a tribute to Hershey at the Hyatt Regency Hotel in Los Angeles, California from April 27th to April 30th, 2000. It was at this convention that the then Chairman of the Joint Chiefs of Staff, General Henry H. Shelton, provided a taped tribute to the veterans, the Medal of Honor, and the relatives of the veterans [n.b. The text of this narration is included at the end of this book].

At the National Japanese Memorial Dedication, Washington, D.C., November 10th, 2000, Hershey was the speaker at the Veteran's breakfast.

Hershey

Hershey

13

At the request of Sherry Thomas, then Chairman of Sunwood Entertainment Corp., the then Chairman of the Joint Chiefs of Staff, General Henry H. Shelton, offered a video-taped tribute to the Japanese-American Korean War Veteran's attendees at the 50th Anniversary of the Korean War Convention, from his Pentagon office.

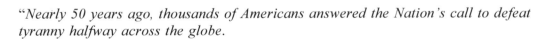

The narrative from this tribute is offered in its entirety for its appropriateness to the telling of this story and as a conclusion to this work, although the courage and the acts, after almost fifty years, that Hiroshi Miyamura demonstrated on the 24th and 25th of April in 1951 still echo down the years. The ripples from his heroic and selfless acts continue to affect an influence upon the consciousness of the world, delivering the message that within us all there resides the potential for greatness, the deep well that exists in all of us that enables us to sacrifice ourselves for our fellow beings.

Now for General Shelton:

> *"Greetings to the Japanese-American Korean War Veterans. The Joint Chiefs and I salute all of you as you gather this week in Los Angeles to renew friendships born in battle and pay tribute to fallen comrades.*

> *"Nearly 50 years ago, thousands of Americans answered the Nation's call to defeat tyranny halfway across the globe.*

Hershey

"Though the Korean War is sometimes called America's forgotten war, the sacrifices made by our Korean War veterans will never be forgotten.

"There would not be the flag of an independent South Korea flying over Seoul today, if not for your service and sacrifice.

"I've been asked to say a few words about the Medal of Honor, and it is an honor and privilege to do so.

"As most of you know, the Medal of Honor is bestowed by the Congress, and it is the highest military decoration our nation can give. Medal of Honor recipients are members of the most select fraternity on earth.

"There are no associate members, no honorary or guest memberships. Membership is not measured by influence, or rank, or civic accomplishment. Membership comes only to those who were touched with fire... whose gallant actions went above and beyond the call of duty, and who risked their lives for comrades and country without reservation or regret.

"Winston Churchill said that of all the human qualities, courage comes first because it is the quality that guarantees all others. The courage that is embodied by the Medal of Honor has for more than 200 years guaranteed our freedom, our security, and our prosperity.

"My message to you today would not be complete without recognizing the families who have also given so much for our nation. Theirs has not been a light nor easy burden. They also bore the risk of war. They risked their fathers and mothers, their brothers and sisters, their sons and daughters, their husbands and wives.

"We owe them a debt of gratitude and honor for their dedication and sacrifice.

"I wish you the very best for this 50th reunion celebration. America is enriched by your legacy of valor which will inspire new generations with the noble virtues of duty, of service, and of courage.

"May God bless the Japanese-American Korea War veterans, and may God bless all who have served and who continue to serve our nation in uniform, and God bless America."

Hershey

Bibliography

1. Video-taped interviews with Hiroshi Miyamura in 1999 and 2000, conducted by Charles R. Woodson, Sherry L. Thomas, and C. Woodson, of Sunwood Entertainment Corp. http://www.sunwoodentertainment.com,in both Gallup, New Mexico and in Southern California.

2. Video-taped interview with family members: older sister Michiko and her husband Paul Yoshida, younger brother Kei, and his wife Kimi, and younger sister Shizuko, conducted by Charles R. Woodson, Sherry L. Thomas, and C. Woodson, of Sunwood Entertainment Corp. http://www.sunwoodentertainment.com, in Southern California in 2000.

3. The story behind the name for Gallup was collected at http://www.ci.gallup.nm.us/shst.htm on August 4th, 2001.

4. The mystery behind the name Gamerco was unveiled at http://www.pagosa.com/4corners/us_666_to_shiprock.html on July 21st 2001.

5. Chalfen, Richard, Turning Leaves: The Photographic Collections of Two Japanese American Families, Albuquerque, New Mexico, University of New Mexico Press, 1991.

6. Transcript of audio-taped interview of Hershey Miyamura, conducted by Michele Dowell for the Rio Grande Historical Collection of Oral Histories of New Mexico State University, on November 21, 1990, conducted at his home in Gallup, New Mexico.

7. Telephone interviews, email, and fax exchanges with: Michiko and Paul Yoshida, Pat Shimamura, Shizuko Tanikawa, Shigeko Sasaki, Momoko Saruwatari, Chiyo Herrera, Hershey and Terry Miyamura, Anna Jean DiGregorio, and Dan L. and Joyce Ann McKinney, all between June, 2001 and March, 2002.

8. Research about Camp Patrick Henry, in Virginia was collected from: www.strandlab.com/forts/patrickhenry.html on October 2nd 2001.

9. Photographs of the return of the 442nd RCT in New York Harbor, and the presentation ceremonies with President Harry S. Truman, captured from military archival film footage in the Sunwood Entertainment film library, by Charles R. Woodson.

10. Search for information about Camp Stoneman in California was successful at: http://www.hnd.usace.army.mil/oew/factshts/factshts/stoneman.pdf on October 2nd 2001.

11. Map of the Chinese Spring Offensive, April 22-30, 1951 gleaned from: http://www.koreanwar.org/html/maps/map32_full.jpg September 9th 2001.

12. Photographs of the military conflict in Korea selected by Charles R. Woodson from military archival footage in the Sunwood Entertainment film library.

13. "Miyamura family awaits return of Korean war hero" A clipping, probably from the Rafu Shimpo, Los Angeles, dated August 21, 1953, Miyamura Family Scrapbooks.

14. "Sgt. Hershey's Midnight Battle" Denver Post, by Bill Hosokawa, Empire Magazine, October 11, 1953, Miyamura Family Scrapbooks.

15. Griffin, W.E.B. The Captains: Brotherhood of War Book II, New York, Jove Books, The Berkley Publishing Group, 1982. Reprinted with permission of the author.

16. The fate of the allied troops, numerically disadvantaged at the Chosen [alternatively

Hershey

spelled "Chosin or Changjin"] Reservoir and their retreat to Hungnam was garnered at http://www.rt66.com/~korteng/SmallArms/chosin.htm on August 29th 2001.

17. Report of the low temperatures at POW Camp 1 vicinity [Chiangsong or alternatively Ch'ang Ni, North Korea, winter 1952-53], reported by: http://www.awm.gov.au/korea/faces/pow/pow.htm gathered on September 10th 2001.

18. "Long-Kept Secret Citation of Medal of Honor Winner Released" Pacific Citizen, August 28, 1953, Los Angeles, Datelined: Washington, Miyamura Family Scrapbooks.

19. "New Mexico Nisei Prisoner Awarded Medal of Honor" Unknown publication, probably a Gallup, NM newspaper, with a byline by Robert Gibson, datelined: Freedom Village, Korea, with no date, Miyamura Family Scrapbooks.

20. "Freed POW safe" Clipping, possibly from the Rafu Shimpo, with a penciled date of August 20, 1953, Miyamura Family Scrapbooks.

21. "Post Time," Denver Post, Empire Magazine, Editorial Page, by Bill Hosokawa, October 11, 1953, Miyamura Family Scrapbooks.

22. "Hiroshi On Way Home" Rafu Shimpo, Los Angeles, August 20, 1953 [n.b. Due to the International Dateline, it was already the 21st of August in Korea], Miyamura Family Scrapbooks.

23. "Freed POW Safe, 3 Sisters Learn Brother is Hero" unattributed, probably Rafu Shimpo, with a penciled date, August 20, 1953, Miyamura Family Scrapbooks.

24. "2 from Cal. Amog [sic] Latest POWs to Be Released" Unattributed clipping, The United Nations Command's official list of American prisoners of war released to freedom today at Pan Mun Jom. Associated Press, dateline Munsan [South Korea], August 20, 1953, was the first mention of Hershey's promotion from Corporal to Sergeant, Miyamura Family Scrapbooks.

25. "Medal of Honor: Death Usual Price for Famous Military Award" Los Angeles Examiner, Sunday, August 23, 1953, by Darrell Garwood, Miyamura Family Scrapbooks.

26. "Li'l Tokio [sic] celebration ends with homage to medalist" Rafu Shimpo, Los Angeles, August 24, 1953, Miyamura Family Scrapbooks.

27. "On Miyamura, Sgt. U.S. Army" Rafu Shimpo, Los Angeles, with a penciled date of "9/1953", Miyamura Family Scrapbooks.

28. Copy of a telegram from Western Union, included in Miyamura Family Scrapbooks.

29. "Medal of Honor winner gets rousing cheer as Marine Adder in port; Gallup readies fete" by Yas Nakanishi, Rafu Shimpo, dateline San Francisco, although a penciled date of September 5, 1953 is on the clipping, the context of the clipping indicates it is dated September 8, 1953, Miyamura Family Scrapbooks.

30. "Hero Leads 367 Captives From Ship" Unattributed clipping, dateline San Francisco, and internally dated September 5 [1953], Miyamura Family Scrapbooks.

31. Information about Hershey being the 62nd winner of the Medal of Honor in the Korean war, conflicts with information contained in: "Medal of Honor: Death Usual Price for Famous Military Award" by Darrell Garwood, Los Angeles Examiner, Sunday, August 23, 1953, Sec. 1, Part A, Page 10, which states that a search of Congressional Medal of Honor records showed that there were 104 recipients awarded the Medal during the

Hershey

Korean war, 71 of which died in the act that garnered the award, Miyamura Family Scrapbooks.

32. Information regarding the incarceration of Japanese-American citizens during the Second World War was collected from: http://www.geocities.com/Athens/8420/main.html accessed June 14, 2001, and http://alterasian.com/internment accessed on September 2, 2001.

33. The following Internet site was a source: http://artmuseum.arizona.edu/mfa/artists/scott/post/post.html for details of Poston, Arizona internment camp, accessed on September 1, 2001.

34. An official Army Internet source lists, with statistics current as of May 13, 1997, a total of 131 Medals of Honor awarded during the Korean War, http://www.army.mil/cmh-pg/mohstats.htm accessed July 19, 2000.

35. "Hero's welcome greets Medal of Honor GI at dockside, home" Pacific Citizen [n.b. publication was an organ of the Japanese-American Citizens League], Los Angeles, with a dateline of San Francisco, September 11, 1953, Miyamura Family Scrapbooks.

36. "Thousands Welcome Miyamura Back Home: Crowds Jam Plaza For Hero's Return" By Hank Stern, Associated Press, reported in The Gallup Independent, Gallup, N.M., September 9, 1953, Miyamura Family Scrapbooks.

37. Information about the F-86 Sabre jet's record of combat in Korea, and the Air Force photograph, was obtained at: http://www.wpafb.af.mil/museum/air_power/ap40.htm on August 3rd 2001.

38. The Air Force photograph of the MIG-15 Fagot was downloaded from: http://www.wpafb.af.mil/museum/air_power/ap42.htm on August 3rd 2001.

39. "A hero comes home to Gallup" by Bill Hosokawa, Unattributed four page clipping [probably The Denver Post], Miyamura Family Scrapbooks.

40. "Huge Turnout for Gallup's Hero" unattributed, undated, Miyamura Family Scrapbooks.

41. "Welcome Home - New Mexico's Hiroshi Miyamura - Medal of Honor Winner" Veterans Voice [New Mexico], September 1953, Photograph, Miyamura Family Scrapbooks.

42. " 'Hershey' Is Honored at JACL Party Here" unattributed, undated, Miyamura Family Scrapbooks.

43. "Governor Hails Miyamura 'Most Outstanding Citizen' " unattributed, undated, Miyamura Family Scrapbooks.

44. "Miyamura Testimonial Banquet Tickets Go On Sale In Little Tokio" [sic], The Los Angeles Nisei Weekly - Crossroads, September 18, 1953, Miyamura Family Scrapbooks.

45. "Two functions await Miyamura's revisit to Los Angeles next week" Rafu Shimpo, September 17, 1953, Miyamura Family Scrapbooks.

46. "Society as I Find It" by Cobina Wright, Los Angeles Times, September 1953, Miyamura Family Scrapbooks.

47. Dinner Menu, September 25, 1953, among assorted souvenirs of the event kept by Mr. & Mrs. Paul Yoshida, Table 1, Miyamura Family Scrapbooks.

48. "CMH awardee paid tribute by Southland residents in testimonial dinner at Statler"

Hershey

unattributed, by Henry Mori, September 26, 1953, Miyamura Family Scrapbooks.

49. "Shy Medal of Honor winner made honorary Arizona citizen at fete" unattributed, datelined Phoenix, Miyamura Family Scrapbooks.

50. "Miyamura trip to Pentagon set" unattributed, datelined Gallup, N.M., Miyamura Family Scrapbooks.

51. "Washington Office, D.C. Chapter Hosts to Medal of Honor Winner" Pacific Citizen, Los Angeles, October 23, 1953, datelined Gallup, N.M., Miyamura Family Scrapbooks.

52. "Sgt. H. Miyamura Named Among 10 Outstanding of '53" unattributed, datelined Tulsa, with no date, Miyamura Family Scrapbooks.

53. "Washington, D.C., CLers honor Medal of Honor Nisei hero at testimonial" Pacific Citizen, date unknown, dateline Washington, Miyamura Family Scrapbooks.

54. "Brother of Downey Business Woman Receives Congressional Medal of Honor from President" unattributed, date unknown, Miyamura Family Scrapbooks.

55. "L.B. [Long Beach, CA] Women's Brother Gets Top Award" unattributed, undated photograph, Miyamura Family Scrapbooks.

56. Information collected about the long history of the Willard Hotel at http://www.livinghistoryonline.com/willard.htm August 2nd, 2001.

57. "Ike Honors 7 Korea War Heroes - White House Event - Gives Medals of Honor", by Associated Press, Los Angeles Herald & Express, October 27, 1953, dateline Washington, Miyamura Family Scrapbooks.

58. "Eisenhower Honors Soldiers of Valor" photograph [Associated Press Wirephoto], Los Angeles Examiner, October 28, 1953, Miyamura Family Scrapbooks.

59. "Ike Pins Honor Medals on Seven Korea Heroes" unattributed, probably Pacific Citizen, dateline Washington (AP), undated, Miyamura Family Scrapbooks.

60. "Eisenhower Present [sic] Medal to Miyamura" unattributed, dateline Washington, undated, Miyamura Family Scrapbooks.

61. "In Tribute to Hiroshi Miyamura, CMH" Pacific Citizen, October 18, 1953, Miyamura Family Scrapbooks.

62. "Sgt. Hiroshi Miyamura" Rafu Shimpo, Los Angeles, no date, accompanies a full-page photograph of Hershey wearing his Medal of Honor, by Toyo Miyatake, Miyamura Family Scrapbooks.

63. Photograph of President Eisenhower shaking Hershey's hand after presentation of the CMOH, New Japanese-American News, Los Angeles, January 1, 1954, Miyamura Family Scrapbooks.

64. "Observation - Ten Top in News" unattributed, undated [but by context either the end of December 1953, or early January 1954], item number three is "Award of Medal of Honor to Sgt. Hiroshi Miyamura" Miyamura Family Scrapbooks.

65. "Sgt. Miyamura's Memorable Week in Washington" probably Pacific Citizen, byline Mike Masaoka, December 18, 1953, with photos, Miyamura Family Scrapbooks.

66. "New Mexico Salons Write to NW Times, Pay High Tribute to Sgt. Miyamura" The Northwest Times [New Mexico], pencilled-in date of January 2, 1954, Miyamura Family Scrapbooks.

Hershey

67. "Miyamuras honored in Seattle" unattributed but probably Pacific Citizen, January 29, 1954, dateline Seattle, Miyamura Family Scrapbooks.

68. "Sgt. Miyamura named 'Young Man of Year' " Rafu Shimpo, Los Angeles, January 4, 1954, Miyamura Family Scrapbooks.

69. "Named Top Ten Young Americans of '53" Unattributed photographs, Associated Press Wirephoto, undated, Miyamura Family Scrapbooks.

70. "Miyamura honored by Utah junior chamber of commerce" unattributed, dateline Salt Lake City, [February 21, 1954], Miyamura Family Scrapbooks.

71. "Honors for Hersh" unattributed, undated, Miyamura Family Scrapbooks.

72. "Hiroshi Miyamura - Winner of the Congressional Medal of Honor - The Nisei salute Hiroshi Miyamura" page from convention brochure [13th Biennial National Convention], Japanese-American Citizens League, Los Angeles, September 2-6, 1954, Miyamura Family Scrapbooks.

73. "300 Mountain-Plain conventioneers honor Nisei Medal of Honor winner" Pacific Citizen, Los Angeles, December 4, 1953, Miyamura Family Scrapbooks.

74. "Medal winner visits Los Angeles confab" unattributed, December 5, 1966. Miyamura Family Scrapbooks.

75. Copy of George Akimoto's painting of Hershey ["Portrait of Hiroshi Miyamura"] obtained from: http://www.homeofheroes.com/profiles/hershey_painting.jpg on September 10th 2001.

76. The details of Madam Butterfly by Puccini were gathered at: http://rick.stanford.edu/opera/Puccini/Butterfly/main.html on September 4th 2001.

77. Facts about Bing Crosby's Sunday, Monday or Always collected at: http://www.kcmetro.cc.mo.us/pennvalley/biology/lewis/crosby/SundayMondayAlways.html on September 4th 2001.

78. Information derived about Colorado Governor Ralph L. Carr was gleaned from: http://www.archives.state.co.us/govs/carr.html#bio and further reaction about the Japanese evacuees from the west coast was obtained from: http://www.du.edu/~anballar/Reactions_of_People_from_Colorado.html on September 4th 2001.

79. Definition of the term Nikkei, located at: http://www.kent.wednet.edu/KSD/SJ/Nikkei/Nikkei_homePage.html on September 5th 2001.

80. Video-taped tribute by General Henry H. Shelton, the then, Chairman of the Joint Chiefs of Staff, provided by his office for presentation at the commemoration of the 50th anniversary of the Korean War by members of the Japanese-American Korean War Veterans at their Los Angeles convention in April of 2000.

81. Photograph and information about General Henry H. Shelton, Chairman of the Joint Chiefs of Staff, was downloaded and accessed at: http://www.dtic.mil/jcs/core/chairman.html on August 13, 2000.

82. Miyamura family photographs collected by C. Woodson and Charles R. Woodson, Sunwood Entertainment Corp. http://www.sunwoodentertainment.com, courtesy of Hershey

Michiko Yoshida from her many scrapbooks kept for the family in March, 2002.

83. Cover art of George Akimoto's painting of Hershey ["Portrait of Hiroshi Miyamura"] used with permission of the Army Art Collection, U.S. Army Center of Military History, April 2002.

84. Photographs of Hershey, Terry, Amelio DiGregorio, and his wife Anna Jean in Europe, courtesy of Anna Jean DiGregorio.

85. Additional photographs of the separation ceremony at Ft. Bliss, and the photograph of Dan L. McKinney and Raymond J. McAuliffe after their release from Camp 1, courtesy of Dan L. McKinney.

86. The uncompromising value of the outstanding Internet aid, Atomica program, available at its website located at: http://www.atomica.com was invaluable in conducting research and checking facts during the writing of this book.

87. Photographs captured, formatted and supplied by Karen Uyematsu, of Karen Uyematsu Design, in Anaheim, California.

ABOUT THE AUTHORS & PUBLISHER

Dale E. Malone an avid reader, poet, writer, and computer-applications guru, has always been fascinated by military history. With his own service during the Vietnam War, he was intrigued with Hershey's tale of patriotism in the face of discrimination. Mr. Malone has been involved in a variety of unique businesses over the years that have broadened his horizons and interests. Though he was raised as a military brat, he still enjoys traveling and immersing himself in new adventures.

Charles R. Woodson is the Executive Producer and CEO of his own entertainment media company. Through a mutual friend, he was introduced to Hershey's story, and was inspired to capture the incredible story on video. Mr. Woodson's life's passion is to capture all the personal stories of veterans on video, and turn those stories into products through graphic novels, books, documentaries, web series, feature films and other media in order to preserve and pass along those stories to future generations.

Sunwood Entertainment Corporation, http://www.sunwoodentertainment.com is a family owned and operated independent production and publishing company, whose purpose is to create, produce, acquire, and distribute, exceptional products that entertain, inspire, motivate, challenge, and educate and make those products available to the world, utilizing the internet.

Hershey

Made in the USA
Coppell, TX
14 February 2023

12702597R00072